lonely planet
food

SPAIN
From the Source

*Authentic recipes from the
people that know them best*

Written by **Sally Davies** and photographed by **Margaret Stepien**

CONTENTS

INTRODUCTION

To a casual observer, there might seem something of a disconnect between the outward face of Spanish gastronomy – the futuristic revolution curated by Ferran Adrià and his ardent, blue-sky disciples – and the largely unchanged way in which the ordinary Spaniard shops, cooks and eats. The countless dishes that can be traced back to the pastoral tradition of carrying bread, oil, vinegar and garlic as sustenance on the long days and weeks of driving sheep to pastures new; the citrus fruits, saffron, cumin and almonds that came with the Moorish invasion; and the fascination with the tomatoes, peppers, corn and potatoes that arrived from the New World in the 16th-century Columbian Exchange. These were the great seismic shifts in Spanish home-cooking, not the advent of foams, freeze-drying, and cooking sous-vide.

Change is afoot, yes, but only insofar as it builds on the love and respect for what has gone before. Phrases such as 'slow food' and 'food miles' are all but redundant here, where the ready meal is an unknown concept and produce is only available for as long as it is in season. Almost every town has its weekly market, where herbs are sold in tied bouquets, where rice and flour come in hessian sacks, where your requested cut of meat is sliced from the animal in front of your eyes, where

potatoes are muddy and apples misshapen. Where chickens have heads.

The rituals, too, continue to be sacred. Families come together on Sundays for animated afternoons centred around paella. An intrinsic part of any neighbourhood fiesta is the setting up of long trestle tables for communally cooked and eaten dinners that go on late into the night. The *matanza*, the annual slaughtering of pigs, followed by days of feasting, is still a reality in hundreds of Spanish villages and towns.

It is exactly these deeply entrenched traditions that provide the springboard for what is happening in restaurant kitchens around the country. Something I heard over and over while researching this book was 'What we're aiming to do is resurrect old recipes but bring them into the present day.' Many of the recipes here reflect that philosophy, in which the spirits of long-passed grandmothers (and it is always grandmothers) provide the guiding hand at the stove, and inform the fundamental combinations and techniques at the heart of every innovation. You'll find dishes that have passed down through generations of a chef's family, but in his or her hands are given a twist: a *fabada asturiana* resembling a Tàpies art installation on the plate; hake given a hint of parsley when fake caviar containing its essence explodes on the tongue. We're not pretending these recipes are simple, but with a little dedication – and perhaps a pipette – these are creations set to impress at a dinner party.

Of course you'll also find good, honest peasant food, of a type that anyone could make with whatever happens to be in the larder – which is exactly the attitude with which it is approached in Spain.

NORTHEAST SPAIN

The Catalans, Valencians and Mallorquíns ploughed their own furrow long before the likes of Ferran Adrià changed the course of global cooking, and molecular gastronomy is an adjunct to fiercely traditional cuisine; sticky stews and paellas, meat and vegetables seared over flames scented with vine branches, and the unlikely pairing of mar i muntanya *(meat with seafood).*

BIKINI DE TARTUFO

Truffled cheese & ham toasted sandwich

A playful take on a longstanding favourite bar snack, celebrity chef Carles Abellan's 'bikini' is also a gourmet delight, given a delicious lift with a hint of truffle.

Legend has it that the curiously named *bikini de tartufo* was first introduced in the 1950s by the owner of storied nightclub Sala Bikini (which itself took its Cold War–era name from US nuclear testing site, the Bikini Atoll), who brought the idea of the croque-monsieur from France. General Franco, who was in power in Spain at the time, had banned the use of foreign names, so it became known as 'the house sandwich'. As its popularity grew throughout Barcelona and Catalunya (where it is still ubiquitous to this day), punters would ask for 'one of those bikini sandwiches'. Eventually the name stuck.

In its most common form, it is nothing but a cheese and ham toasted sandwich, but Michelin-starred chef Carles Abellan has succeeded in taking it to a whole new level at his playful, neo-traditional tapas bar, Tapas 24.

'Everyone thinks I invented this,' he laughs, 'but I stole the idea from Ferran Adrià when I worked at El Bulli. We served it at a banquet we were catering in the late '80s, and it was a huge success. You now see it everywhere, but it's important to get it right – you have to be generous with the ingredients. You can use regular white sliced bread, but we use tramezzino for the best texture. *Mozzarella di bufala* (buffalo mozzarella) is expensive, truffle is expensive, *jamón ibérico* is expensive. This is an expensive sandwich. But the mozzarella makes it light, sweet and creamy, in a counterpoint to the saltiness of the ham. The truffle takes it to another level.'

'There are some dishes that are timeless,' Carles says. 'We had them as children, and the flavours stay engraved in your memory. They also taste as good now as they did fifty years ago. The bikini is one of these.'

Chef //
Carles Abellan
Location //
Tapas 24, Barcelona

BIKINI DE TARTUFO
Truffled cheese & ham toasted sandwich

Serves 4

Preparation & cooking time 15min

*4 slices tramezzino (or 8 slices of white bread,
    without crusts)*
200g (7oz) mozzarella di bufala
pinch of salt
truffle oil, to taste
80g (3oz) jamón ibérico, finely sliced
50g (1¾oz) melted butter

1 Cut the bread in half if using tramezzino.
Thickly slice the mozzarella, patting dry
with kitchen paper, and lay on half the bread.
Lightly sprinkle with salt and drizzle with
truffle oil.

2 Lay the *jamón ibérico* on top of the cheese,
followed by the second slice of bread.

3 Brush both sides of the bread with melted
butter and toast in a sandwich toaster
until golden.

ESCALIVADA
Chargrilled vegetable salad

Smoky, chargrilled vegetables, torn into strips and served cool with olive oil, are the preferred Catalan accompaniment to roast meat, or simply served on tomato-rubbed bread and topped with anchovies.

Some have argued that the *escalivada* is merely a deconstructed ratatouille (many Catalan dishes do have a French overtone), but history tells us that red peppers, aubergines (eggplants) and tomatoes were used in Catalunya long before they crossed the border into France.

The onions most commonly used are *cebollas tiernas* (tender onions), known as 'green onions' elsewhere, though any reasonably sweet onion will serve. This dish is best made in summer, when the other vegetables are in season and at the high point of flavour, but can be made all year round.

'Traditionally, the vegetables are cooked over the embers,' says Fidel Amigó, who runs the family restaurant with his brother Santi. 'In fact the word *escalivada* is Catalan for "roasted in embers", but I prefer them cooked in the flames. It gives them a deeper, smokier quality, especially the aubergine. The kind of wood you use makes a difference, too. Here we're in wine country, so we can use vine shoots, which add a lot to the flavour, but are quick to burn, so we also use oak.'

The *brasa*, the long wood-fired grill that sits at the entrance to the kitchen, is the heart and soul of Cal Xim. Everything is thrown on it, not just the lamb, chicken and rabbit that makes up the best part of demand, but fish and even foie gras is seared and made aromatic over this roaring blaze. It lends the restaurant a homely, comforting smell, perfectly in keeping with animated chatter of regulars and the traffic of their children barrelling in and out between the dining room and the playground outside. 'It's always been like this,' says Santi. 'We get a lot of wine tourists now, but at heart it's still the same neighbourhood bar my parents set up in 1974.'

Chef //
Fidel Amigó
Location //
Cal Xim, Sant Pau d'Ordal

ESCALIVADA
Chargrilled vegetable salad

Serves 4–6

Preparation & cooking time 30min

2 large red peppers
3 medium tomatoes
2 aubergines (eggplants)
2 medium onions
sprinkle of salt
olive oil to drizzle on top

1 Simply roast everything whole over a flame – a barbecue is ideal, but a gas ring also works well – until the outside layer is completely carbonised and the flesh is soft.

2 Remove this layer (the easiest way to peel the peppers and tomatoes is to seal them in a plastic bag for 15 minutes and let the steam loosen the skin), slice the aubergines lengthways, tomatoes and onions and then rip up the sliced aubergine and peppers by hand into strips.

3 Arrange on a plate, sprinkle with salt and drizzle with olive oil. If you make this in advance, take it out of the fridge a couple of hours before serving. It is best served at room temperature.

Tip

This is often served with the Catalan favourite, pa amb tomàquet (bread with tomato) – slices of lightly toasted rustic bread, rubbed with halves of garlic cloves and very ripe tomatoes, then drizzled with olive oil and sprinkled with sea salt.

COQUES
Mallorquín flatbreads

The secret to these little Balearic pizzas is in the flour, says María Solivellas, ardent campaigner for a return to organic and healthier produce and standard-bearer for the Slow Food movement.

'We used to have much more of a rural community on Mallorca,' says María Solivellas, chef and owner of Ca na Toneta, in the tiny village of Caimari, 'but with tourism everyone moved out to the coastal regions or to Palma. This is changing in recent years, with an appetite to live more healthily and honestly.'

María herself has spearheaded many of these changes, with her ceaseless energy channelled into preserving endangered, heritage species from the island, such as the *tap de cortí* pepper. This aromatic little capsicum is indigenous to the Balearics, but had been long-forgotten until a massive campaign led by María and others generated a revival in its production. And now its powdered form, a type of paprika, is found all over the island. Another of her pet projects is *xeixa*, an ancient, unmodified wheat varietal that still grows locally and, ground in the island's one remaining stone mill, preserves all its vital nutrients. 'It's stronger, better for your health and is less likely to provoke allergies,' she says.

This is what she uses for her famed *coques*, unleavened bread bases for any number of toppings. 'It's become our signature product in the restaurant. We've been making them for years, based on old recipes but with the odd tweak to make them lighter, healthier and with more variety. What we did was take out the animal fat (lard) and replace it with extra virgin olive oil, and made a thinner version than the traditional version. This has been our street food for centuries – you can eat it for breakfast, lunch or dinner.'

'The *coca* has infinite possibilities, and every country has their own version, though no one has had quite the success of the Italians and their pizzas,' she laughs.

Chef //
María Solivellas
Location //
Ca na Toneta, Caimari

COQUES
Mallorquín flatbreads

Serves 6

*Preparation & cooking time 30min
plus 30min for making coca dough*

**For the Coca de higos y sobrassada
(Coca with figs & sobrassada sausage)**

1 tsp fresh yeast
75ml (2½ fl oz) extra virgin olive oil
pinch of salt
75ml (2½ fl oz) mineral water, lukewarm
100g (3½oz) white xeixa & 100g (3½oz)
 wholemeal xeixa, or 100g (3½oz) white
 flour & 100g (3½oz) spelt wholemeal flour
 (note: amount of flour is approximate
 & more/less may be added as dough is
 needed)
350g (12oz) onions, finely diced
2 tbsp olive oil, for frying
4 fresh figs, sliced
25g (1oz) sobrassada (a soft, spreadable
 Mallorcan sausage)

**For the Coca de picornells
(Coca with chanterelle mushrooms)**

2 strips of pancetta, chopped
200g (7oz) chanterelle mushrooms (or
 similar meaty mushroom), chopped
2 cloves of garlic, chopped finely

For the Coca de higos y sobrassada (Coca with figs & sobrassada sausage)

1 Pre-heat the oven to 180°C (350°F).
To make the dough, mix the yeast, olive oil and a pinch of salt with the lukewarm water in a large bowl.

2 Add the flour slowly, kneading until it forms a compact and elastic dough. Make sure it doesn't stick to the sides of the bowl.

3 Cover with a cloth, and leave in a warm place to rise (generally about 30 minutes).

4 For the topping, gently fry the onions over a low heat in the olive oil until caramelised (about 15 minutes). Set aside.

5 Divide the pastry into six sections and roll each section into a ball.

6 Roll out each ball into a long, narrow oval shape. You won't need to dust the surface with flour, or oil the baking tray, because this dough is very elastic and shouldn't stick.

7 Spread a thin layer of caramelised onion onto the dough.

8 Top with slices of fig, and dot each fig slice with a little *sobrassada*.

9 Bake the *coques* in the oven at 180°C (350°F) until the base is golden. Serve warm.

For the Coca de picornells (Coca with chanterelle mushrooms)

1 Follow the recipe above from steps 1 through to the end of 7.

2 Sauté the pancetta in a frying pan, until it has released all the fat. Add the mushrooms and the garlic. Stir constantly, on a medium heat, until the ingredients are golden.

3 Spread the mixture on top of the layer of caramelised onions, and bake as above.

Tip

Covered with cling film, the dough can stay in the fridge for up to three days before use.

XATÓ CON PANECILLO DE ALFORFÓN

Salt cod salad with buckwheat bread

A dish so beloved to Catalans that it merits an annually appointed 'ambassador', this salt cod salad holds all its secrets in a spicy almond and hazelnut dressing.

Chef //
Fina Puigdevall
Location //
Les Cols, Olot

Nothing quite prepares you for Les Cols. A sign pointing to the restaurant sits on the side of an unmemorable road lined with showrooms and warehouses, on the outskirts of Olot. There, at the end of a leafy track, a beautiful wisteria-draped *masía* – the typical Catalan farmhouse of stout walls, arcaded porch and an upper loggia – heaves suddenly into view. This is only the first surprise. Inside this rural idyll, the dining room is other-worldly. Something Stanley Kubrick could barely have imagined, it is a long futuristic space where everything, but everything, is gold – the walls, the table, the chairs, even the floor and ceiling shimmer.

The building is where chef Fina Puigdevall's family has lived, in her words, 'forever'. Her mother still lives on the first floor, and Fina's brother and his family above that. In 1990 it was young Fina's dream to open a restaurant and the family went along with it to humour her. 'That's why the entrance is round the back of the house,' she laughs. 'They wouldn't let me in the front, they said it would never catch on.' Fifteen years later, Fina received her first Michelin star, her second in 2010, and is one of the most respected chefs in the country.

For all the fireworks, however, good, honest, Catalan cooking is still at the heart and soul of what Fina does, and for that reason she was elected 'Ambassador of Xató', a title awarded by an association of *xató* aficionados in the Penedès region, south of Barcelona in recognition of services to this dish of crispy endive (chicory), salt cod, tuna, anchovies and a nutty, spicy sauce. Previous incumbents of the title include Joan Roca, chef at what is considered to be the best restaurant in the world, Celler de Can Roca, along with gastronomic game-changer Ferran Adrià.

XATÓ CON PANECILLO DE ALFORFÓN
Salt cod salad with buckwheat bread

Serves 6

Preparation & cooking time 1hr,
not including pre-soaking of salt cod

For the bread
100g (3½oz) fresh yeast
800g (1¾lb) wholewheat flour
200g (7oz) buckwheat
100g (3½oz) lard
15g (½oz) bread improver (optional)
20g (¾oz) salt
50g (1¾oz) sugar
500ml (17½ fl oz) water

For the sauce
pinch of salt
100g (3½oz) almonds
80g (2¾oz) hazelnuts
half a medium onion, roasted (ideally over a
  barbecue)
1 ñora pepper (if ñora is not available, use roasted
  red pepper)
½ tsp pimentón dulce (sweet paprika)
½ tsp pimentón picante (spicy paprika)
1 slice of fried bread
half a head of garlic, roasted (ideally over a
  barbecue)
3 medium tomatoes, roasted (ideally over a
  barbecue)
50ml (1¾ fl oz) olive oil
1 tbsp vinegar

For the xató
2 heads of endive (chicory)
salt & pepper, to taste
120g (4¼oz) salt cod (pre-soaked overnight to
  remove the salt)
120g (4¼oz) cooked tuna (or good-quality tinned)
4 anchovy fillets
80g (2¾oz) olives

1 Preheat the oven to 200°C (390°F).

2 Add a couple of spoonfuls of warm water to the yeast to let it ferment.

3 Meanwhile, to make the bread dough, mix the other ingredients by hand until a smooth dough forms (around 10 minutes) and then add the fermented yeast. Knead the bread for another 10 minutes and then leave to rest for 5 minutes.

4 Divide the dough into portions of about 50g (1¾oz) and roll into balls. Let the dough balls proof until doubled in size and bake for 10 minutes on a tray in the oven. Reserve for later to fill with the *xató*.

5 Make the sauce using a pestle and mortar. Put the salt in the mortar, and then add the other ingredients in the following order: first the almonds, then the hazelnuts (crush well to get a fine paste), then add the onion, the ñora pepper, the two kinds of paprika, the slice of fried bread, garlic, tomatoes, olive oil, and, finally, vinegar.

6 To make the *xató*, put the washed endive leaves in a bowl and season with salt and pepper. Mix in the cod, tuna, anchovies and olives, and then coat lightly in the sauce.

7 Slice off the tops of each of the bread rolls (keep the tops), and hollow out the centre. Fill the hollow with the *xató*, and then place the top of the bread roll back on.

SUQUET
Fish & potato stew

Barcelona's former fishing neighbourhood is home to family-run Suquet de l'Almirall – its version of the eponymous fish and potato stew is as rich and rewarding as you'll find anywhere.

M anel Marqués has worked in his family's restaurant, alongside his brother Quim, since it opened in 1991. In that time, many of the great and the good of Catalan society and beyond have passed through these doors, and dozens of them – from Jean Paul Gaultier to Lou Reed via Woody Allen and Jon Bon Jovi – have left little sketches behind them, which now adorn the deep blue walls.

The restaurant pays homage to the surrounding maritime neighbourhood of Barceloneta, and its dishes reflect the time-honoured customs of local fishers – none more so than the *suquet* that gives the restaurant its name. 'This is primordial cooking from the sea itself,' says Manel. 'It became popular in the '50s, but originated in the stew that the fishermen would cook themselves while out on the waves for long stretches. They would use the fish that would be hard to sell for whatever reason, because it was too bony, or misshapen. They would use iron pots that wouldn't easily tip over with the swaying of the boats and were impossible to break. We try and do the same.'

This faithfulness to the dish's past extends to the use of culinary seawater, favoured over salt by Spanish chefs for what they see as its low sodium chloride and high mineral content. Whether this is true or not – the science is still inconclusive – there is no doubt that it infuses the dish with a briny, elemental flavour, appropriate for a dish whose name comes from the Catalan *suquejar*, to 'bring out the juice'.

In this case 'bringing out the juice' refers to the flavour of the fish – Manel uses rascasse, or scorpion fish, adding 'you can use gilt-head bream, gurnard, stargazer, monkfish, whatever stands up to 20 minutes' cooking' – to infuse the cooking liquid, but it could just as easily refer to bringing out the essence of the sea itself.

Chef //
Manel Marqués
Location //
Suquet de l'Almirall, Barcelona

SUQUET
Fish & potato stew

Serves 6

**Preparation & cooking time 40min,
not including time to prep fish stock**

splash of olive oil
4 Kennebec potatoes (or any waxy potatoes), diced
2 ripe tomatoes, grated
125ml (4½ fl oz) white wine
*1½L (2½ pt) fumet or fish stock (made with the
head & bones of the fish)*
*2½kg (5lb 8oz) red scorpion fish (or gurnard/
monkfish), filleted & de-boned*
1 bunch parsley, finely chopped
2 cloves of garlic, finely chopped
8 prawns
*125ml (4½ fl oz) of purified sea water (or lightly
salted water)*
2 tbsp alioli (garlic mayonnaise, see p264)
salt & pepper, to taste

1 Put a generous splash of olive oil in a cast iron saucepan, and sauté the potatoes for 3 minutes over a high heat.

2 Add the grated tomatoes to the pan, followed immediately by the white wine and let the mixture reduce for a couple of minutes.

3 Pour over the fish stock and cook for 5 minutes.

4 Add the fish fillets, then the chopped herbs and garlic, and cook for another 5 minutes.

5 Add the prawns, then put the lid on the saucepan, reduce the heat to low, and cook for another 10 minutes.

6 Add the sea water and the *alioli*.

7 Adjust seasoning to taste, and serve.

Tip

Lightly roasting the tomatoes before adding them to the potatoes will add a deeper, sweeter flavour.

SÍPIA AMB MANDONGUILLES
Squid with meatballs

Marrying the bounty of the sea with the produce of the pasture, farms and woodland is a peculiarly Catalan speciality, and nowhere does it with more aplomb than traditional taberna Can Pineda.

Originating in the windswept region of the Empordà, north of Barcelona, the tradition of *mar i muntanya* (sea and mountain), in which seafood is cooked alongside meat as part of the same dish, has come to be one of Catalunya's great contributions to Spanish food. One or other of its combinations is always found at Can Pineda, an unassuming neighbourhood restaurant that was created in 1904 and is at odds with the high-rise residential district that has grown around it. Its chef, Jaume Jovells, has run the kitchen for the last 40 years.

To compare *mar i muntanya* to surf and turf is to do it a terrible injustice. The Catalan version has little in common with the steakhouse-style protein overloads of lobster and sirloin, and everything to do with harmony. The piscine element is not a mere sideshow, gracing the edge of the plate, but is brought fully into it, the flavours combining through the binding agents of *sofregit* (see p265) or, in this case, *picada*. These are the cornerstones of Catalan cuisine, the first – nothing more complicated than tomatoes and onions caramelised in olive oil on a very low heat – forming a base for dozens of local dishes, while *picada* adds texture as well as a deep, nutty, herbed and garlicky flavour.

In the case of this dish, it lends a velvety feel and almost chocolatey taste that feels unimaginably opulent for something so apparently simple. Jaume insists it's simply a case of selecting the right ingredients, 'and the rest is practice – it's no good just reading about the principles. Once you learn how to do something properly in the kitchen, you'll never do it badly again. I'm 65 now, it's time to learn something else. I thought I might learn how to use a computer.'

Chef //
Jaume Jovells
Location //
Can Pineda, Barcelona

SÍPIA AMB MANDONGUILLES
Squid with meatballs

Serves 4

Preparation & cooking time 2hr

For the meatballs
1 slice white bread, crusts removed
water or milk to moisten bread
250g (9oz) pork mince
250g (9oz) beef mince
1 tsp salt
2 cloves garlic, finely chopped
3 eggs
small bunch parsley, finely chopped
2 tbsp flour

For the squid
1 large onion, finely chopped
300g (10½ oz) squid
pinch of salt
75ml (2½ fl oz) white wine
2 medium tomatoes, peeled, deseeded and
  finely chopped
½ tsp sugar
olive oil for frying
500ml (17½ fl oz) meat or fish stock (see p265)

1 To make the meatballs, crumble the bread into crumbs, wet with just enough water or milk to moisten, then squeeze out excess liquid.

2 Work the breadcrumbs, pork and beef mince, salt, garlic, eggs and parsley together with your hands, cover and leave for one hour.

3 In a wide, heavy-bottomed saucepan fry the onion on a low heat for 10 minutes. Meanwhile, clean and chop the squid into chunks and sprinkle with salt. Add half of the white wine to the onions and cook for a further 2 minutes, add tomatoes and sugar and cook for another 5 minutes, stirring occasionally.

4 Roll the meat into balls the size of large golf balls, coat in flour and fry them in olive oil for added colour.

5 Fry the squid in olive oil and the rest of the white wine.

6 Add the stock to the onion and tomatoes and simmer for 5 minutes. Add the squid and meatballs, place the lid on the pan and simmer for a further 20 minutes, until the squid is soft.

7 Make the *picada* (see p265) and add to the squid and meatballs and cook for another 20 minutes, remove the lid towards the end to reduce the liquid a little.

POCHAS ESTOFADAS DE LAS POCHOLAS

Las Pocholas bean stew

Alex Múgica recounts the tender tale of philanthropy and sisterhood that lies behind this fragrant stew of creamy Navarran beans and fresh spring vegetables.

On the wall of Alex Múgica's Pamplona restaurant, there is a large black-and-white photo of nine immaculately dressed women, evidently sisters, probably taken in the 1940s. These are Las Pocholas (*pochola* means 'little angel' or 'sweet girl'), for whom this restaurant was named until that incarnation closed in 2000. On his menu, Alex dedicates a handful of dishes to these exceptional women, using recipes that they once used, and tells a wonderful story of how the restaurant came about.

It was their mother's dying wish, he says, that they stay together, open a business and look after one another. They managed this with the financial assistance of friends and neighbours, and ended up not only looking after each other, but paying society back by looking after its less fortunate, feeding them from the restaurant's kitchen and giving them employment whenever the opportunity arose. 'It was not just about the love they put into preparing these dishes,' says Alex, 'but the way they treated the customers and the people around them.' He tells the story of Paquita, a 25-year-old woman whose husband left her in charge of two small children. 'She came to the door looking for help,' he says, 'and Josefina, one of the sisters, said to her, "Paquita, you don't need to worry about a thing. As long as I live, there will be work for you in this restaurant." There are a thousand such stories.'

'This recipe goes back to those days,' he says. 'And has been a classic of Navarra cuisine for even longer. Chefs play about with it – in smarter restaurants, for example, they might add clams – but here we stick with the authentic recipe. Nothing symbolises Pamplona cooking like this one, and it's still the traditional dish for the *Sanfermines* [the annual bull-running festival].'

Chef //
Alex Múgica
Location //
La Cocina de Alex
Múgica, Pamplona

POCHAS ESTOFADAS DE LAS POCHOLAS

Las Pocholas bean stew

Serves 4

Preparation & cooking time 1hr

50ml (1¾ fl oz) olive oil with two cloves of
  sliced garlic
1 onion
1 green pepper
1 carrot
2 tomatoes
1kg (2¼lb) shelled pochas (alternatively use
  cannellini or haricot beans)
3 whole cloves of garlic, peeled
pinch of salt
pinch of sugar
1 tbsp chives, finely chopped, to garnish
12 guindillas (pickled chilli peppers)

1 Fry two cloves of sliced garlic in 50ml (1¾fl oz) of olive oil, and remove the garlic. Reserve the garlic-infused oil.

2 Peel and chop the onion, green pepper, carrot, and two tomatoes into large pieces (so that it will be easy to remove them once cooked).

3 Put the beans in a large saucepan with the three whole garlic cloves, the salt, the chopped vegetables and tomatoes, and cover with water. Bring to the boil, then reduce the heat and simmer for about 20 minutes.

4 Remove the vegetables, garlic cloves and tomato pieces from the beans, puree them and return them to the saucepan.

5 Bring the mixture to the boil and add the garlic-infused oil.

6 Add a pinch of sugar and stir.

7 Garnish with chopped chives and serve with *guindillas*.

Tip

To make the stew thicker and to intensify the flavour, you can add 80g (3oz) of chopped pancetta with the vegetables and tomatoes, and also blend it into a paste with them.

FIDEUÀ
Seafood with noodles

The fideuá has much in common with paella, and is a much-loved leisurely Sunday tradition. This version from Catalan chef Jordi Artal is all at once sticky, chewy and crunchy.

Chef //
Jordi Artal
Location //
Cinc Sentits, Barcelona

Born in Toronto to a Catalan mother, chef Jordi Artal has always closely identified with Spain, even while growing up in Canada. His Barcelona restaurant is a Michelin-starred paean to the traditional dishes of the region, rendered in whimsical interpretations that bring them bang up to date. '*Fideuà* isn't something we'd make as a stand-alone dish at Cinc Sentits,' he says. 'But we do sometimes use it as a component within a dish.'

Something akin to a paella, where noodles take the place of rice, *fideuà* was originally created in Gandía, south of Valencia. 'There are so many stories about how it came about,' says Jordi. 'Some say it's a pasta influence dating back to when the Països Catalans incorporated a tiny pocket of Sardinia, but there is a much quainter story about a fishing crew whose captain would eat more than his fair share of the *arròs a banda* [a similar dish made with rice, see p65] that they used to make on board. The ship's cook substituted the rice for noodles so that the captain wouldn't like it so much and would eat less.'

Jordi is adamant that the recipe is less daunting than it might appear. 'It's almost entirely things that can be made in advance. Then you just throw it together. But the elements themselves are important, especially the *sofrito* (see p265) and the shellfish broth. The broth needs to be really strongly flavoured, so if you're starting with something light then reduce, reduce, reduce. We use a lot of *sofrito*, too, more than in most restaurants. If you use less, the noodles stand up like little soldiers when it comes out of the oven, which looks good and helps to toast the noodles a bit, but the extra *sofrito* gives it much deeper flavour.'

FIDEUÀ
Seafood with noodles

Serves 4

Preparation & cooking time 3hr

Note: larger quantites of the sofrito and
picada components are listed here than are
required for the final fideuà serving. Both can
be frozen for later use.

For the calamari sofrito

3 heads garlic
750g (1½lb) calamari, cleaned
75ml (2½ fl oz) olive oil
15g (½oz) salt
1kg (2¼lb) sweet onion, peeled and finely
   chopped
500g (1lb) tomatoes, peeled, seeded &
   finely chopped
50g (1¾oz) ñora pepper pulp (if ñora is not
   available, use roasted red pepper)
salt & pepper, to taste

For the calamari sofrito

1 Wrap each garlic head in aluminium foil and bake at 175°C (350°F) until very soft. Set aside to cool slightly, then scrape out the pulp with a spoon and set aside.

2 Chop the calamari bodies and tentacles in ½cm (¼in) cubes.

3 Heat a large cast-iron pan over medium-high heat until smoking hot. Do not add any oil to the pan. Once the pan is hot, add all of the calamari at once and spread it out. It will start to sputter.

4 Leave the calamari to char in the pan, without moving it. It will release liquid that will then evaporate and the squid will begin to toast on the sides. At this point you can scrape the pan with a metal scraper to move the calamari around.

5 Once all the liquid in the pan is gone and the calamari is toasted on the edges, add the olive oil, salt, and onion.

6 Lower heat to medium-low and cook until the onion is golden brown. Add the chopped tomato and cook over a low heat for 2 hours. If the mixture starts to dry out or catch on the bottom, add some more olive oil or water.

7 Add the ñora pepper pulp and the garlic pulp and simmer for another 30 minutes. Adjust seasoning to taste.

For the fideuà noodles

1 head garlic
80g (2¾oz) fideuà noodles (size no.1)

For the garlic-parsley picada

75g (2½oz) parsley leaves
200ml (7 fl oz) olive oil
15g (½oz) stale or fried bread
15g (½oz) sliced garlic cloves
½ tsp salt

For the fideuà

600ml (1pt) strong shellfish stock
80g (2¾oz) toasted fideuà noodles
25g (1oz) calamari sofrito
10–15g (⅓–½oz) garlic-parsley picada
salt & pepper, to taste
alioli (see p264), to serve

For the fideuà noodles

1 Crush the garlic and stir into the noodles.

2 Place on a baking sheet and bake at 180°C (350°F), stirring every few minutes, until golden brown.

For the garlic-parsley picada

1 Place everything in a blender and process at high speed until smooth.

To assemble the fideuà

1 Bring the shellfish stock to simmer in a pan. Put the noodles in a 4-serving paella pan with the *sofrito* and heat over a medium heat for a minute or two.

2 Pour in the stock all at once and cook over medium-high heat until almost all the liquid has been absorbed by the noodles.

3 Stir in the *picada*, adjust the seasoning, then place in a hot oven for 1–2 minutes until the edges are toasted. Serve with *alioli* on the side.

'Sofrito, or sofregit, is one of the Catalan mother sauces, made from slow-cooked onions, tomatoes, and olive oil. It is the base of too many dishes to count, without countless recipes that begin with "first, make a sofregit"... Similar or equivalent sauces exist in almost all the Mediterranean cuisines.'

Jordi Artal

POLLO AL CHILINDRÓN

Chicken with peppers & tomatoes

Juan José Banqueri has made it his mission to rediscover and reinvent old recipes, but here he sticks with a faithful rendition of the typically Aragonese chicken stew.

Watered by the tributaries of the River Ebro, the valleys of Aragón are a fertile seam for growing vegetables, and many of its dishes reflect that. The *chilindrón* (usually made with chicken, but occasionally with lamb or pork) came about when the conquistadores returned from the Americas, bringing with them peppers and tomatoes (though the use of tomato is somewhat disputed among the Aragonese). Centuries ago, it was eaten at family and community gatherings, and it is thought that its name might come from the card game – *chilindrón* – that was frequently played at these events, particularly in the 17th century.

'This recipe is very traditional,' says Juan José Banqueri, 'and we've stayed faithful to the original. There are lots of things you can do to it, but it's tasty as it is. The important thing is to find a good chicken. A free-range chicken is a whole different kettle of fish from a battery-farmed chicken, it's a different sort of meat.'

Juanjo, as he is known, manages the kitchen, while his wife Maite works the front of house. 'We started out as a very traditional restaurant,' she says, 'but it's evolved over time and we do both ancient and modern versions of the same dish.'

'The idea of the restaurant is to find old recipes and bring them up to date, using local produce whenever we can,' says Juanjo. 'This chicken, for example, we get from a producer near Huesca, in a town called Poleñino, which is famous for the quality of its chickens. They have a longer life and get more exercise, so the flesh becomes darker and a little less tender. It takes a little longer to cook – up to two hours, while ordinary chicken takes half an hour – but has much more taste.'

Chef //
Juan José Banqueri Fernández
Location //
Parrilla Albarracín,
Señora del Carmen

POLLO AL CHILINDRÓN
Chicken with peppers and tomatoes

Serves 4–6

Preparation & cooking time 1hr

2–3 tbsp olive oil, for frying
6 cloves of garlic, peeled
1 free-range chicken, cut into 6 or 8 pieces
1 medium onion, diced
500g (1lb) ripe tomatoes, peeled & chopped
2 red peppers, roasted & skin removed, then chopped
2 bay leaves
a sprig of rosemary
a sprig of thyme
125ml (4½ fl oz) white wine
salt & pepper to taste
200g (7oz) Teruel or other boiled ham, chopped,
* plus a ham bone (optional)*

1 Heat the olive oil in a large saucepan, and gently fry five of the whole garlic cloves. Remove the garlic and set aside.

2 Fry the chicken in the olive oil until golden, then remove.

3 Sauté the onion until it is translucent, then add the tomatoes, peppers, the remaining clove of garlic (chopped), the bay leaves, rosemary, thyme, salt and pepper to taste, and the ham bone (if using).

4 Add the wine, and allow to reduce (15 minutes or so) on a medium heat.

5 Add the chicken pieces and the chopped ham. Simmer slowly until the chicken is tender and is coming away from the bone (about 30–45 minutes).

6 Remove the ham bone (if using), and serve.

LUBINA A LA MALLORQUINA

Mallorcan-style sea bream

Hidden behind the thick forbidding walls of a former training school for missionaries, Simply Fosh is all space and light, and utterly Mediterranean – with dishes to match.

Chef //
Marc Fosh
Location //
Simply Fosh, Palma

When Marc opened Simply Fosh, his idea – as the name suggests – was to keep it simple, casual, unpretentious. He stated that his intentions were to provide great food at pocket-friendly prices and in a relaxed environment, but that he and his staff had no desire to go chasing Michelin stars. As things turned out, the Michelin critics had other ideas, and were soon to recognise the restaurant in their lists.

Having grown up in London, and spent time in some of its higher-echelon kitchens, Marc had a stint in Paris and then ended up in San Sebastián, working at triple-starred Berasategui. After all his classical training, he was surprised and delighted at the Spanish way of doing things; olive oil instead of butter and cream, and an emphasis on lighter, less rich food. When he finally opened his own restaurant in Palma, this was his focus – healthier, simpler food with no bells and whistles, and lots of local produce. The space at Simply Fosh, with floor-to-ceiling glass around a bright patio, reflects this mood, as does the presence of Marc himself, who wanders around greeting diners like old friends, determined, as he says, to break down the barriers between kitchen and dining room.

'I fell in love with classic Spanish cuisine a long time ago,' he says, 'but sometimes felt that the ingredients were so overcooked that the dish lost its identity.' His mission is to recreate dishes like this simple sea bream *a la Mallorquina*, with potatoes, tomatoes, raisins and pine nuts, but with slightly untraditional methods and replacing the bed of fried potatoes with a light, foamy puree. 'In this recipe we separated all ingredients and put them together at the end, trying to respect all the ingredients by serving them at their optimum cooking point, to retain all the flavour and freshness.'

LUBINA A LA MALLORQUINA
Mallorcan-style sea bream

Serves 4

Preparation & cooking time 1hr

For the dressing
50ml (1¾ fl oz) sherry vinegar
30g (1oz) raisins
20g (¾oz) pine nuts, lightly toasted
100g (3½oz) tomatoes, peeled & chopped
100g (3½oz) sundried tomatoes, finely chopped
200ml (7fl oz) olive oil
2 tbsp finely chopped parsley
salt & pepper, to taste

For the potato puree
350g (12¼oz) potatoes, peeled & chopped
100g (3½oz) onion, chopped
800ml (1½pt fish stock)
300ml (10½ fl oz) olive oil
salt & pepper, to taste

For the sea bream
3 tbsp olive oil
4 x 150g (5¼oz) sea bream fillets, skin on
handful spinach leaves
4 spears samphire (if available,
  otherwise asparagus)

1 Pre-heat the oven to 180°C (350°F).

2 To make the dressing, bring the sherry vinegar to a boil in a saucepan. Add the raisins and take off the heat. Let the raisins cool in the vinegar. When cool, add the pine nuts, both the fresh and sundried tomatoes, olive oil and parsley, and season.

3 Meanwhile, cook the potatoes and the onion in the fish stock for about 15-20 minutes. Add the olive oil and blend. Pass through a sieve, and adjust seasoning to taste.

4 For the sea bream, heat the olive oil in a frying pan. Fry the sea bream fillets with the skin sides down until they are golden and crunchy. Remove fillets from the oil, and put them on a tray in the oven for 4 minutes.

5 To serve, arrange the sea bream fillets in four deep dishes. Wilt a handful of spinach leaves in a frying pan, and place over the top. Pour over a spoonful of the dressing. Serve with the potato puree. Garnish with samphire/asparagus.

Tip

Before making the puree, leave the potatoes to rest in a little olive oil for 20 minutes, which intensifies the flavour.

PAELLA VALENCIANA
Chicken & rabbit paella

Valencia, surrounded by paddy fields, orchards and vegetable gardens, is the crucible of Spain's best-known contribution to world cuisines, and the paella valenciana is the prototype for a hundred variations.

'Everything most famous about Valencian cooking – oranges, lemons, saffron, tiger nuts –is thanks to the Arabic influence,' says José Manuel Benito, chef at Arrocería La Valenciana. 'The Moors brought rice over with them in the 8th century, and that's where it began, and the risotto was invented seven centuries later. This bomba rice is from the Albufera, 3km from here – Valencia is in a valley, where two rivers meet, so there's plenty of water and the land is very fertile, so vegetables have been grown here since Roman times. Everything we use in this dish comes from nearby, from the beans to the snails.'

Many Valencians will insist that this version is the only paella (chicken, rabbit, beans) that should bear the name, and that those containing seafood, or – horror of horrors – a mix of seafood and meat, are merely *arroces* (rice dishes).

The best way to cook a paella is on a barbecue. This is to ensure that the rice cooks evenly and that there is a healthy *socarrat* – the crunchy layer that forms on the bottom and is a prized treat eaten with the fingers, much as shards of crackling are to a pork roast. Valencians often use wide, specially made gas burners, but another solution is to use the broadest pan you can find and gradually rotate it over two, three or four burners on a hob.

Named for the pan in which it is cooked and served, which itself comes from the Latin *patella* (a large shallow bowl used for feasts or sacrifices in ancient times), paella is often described as an activity as much as a dish. It's intended for long, leisurely lunches with family or friends, and the proper, sociable, way to eat it is with a wooden spoon directly from the shared pan.

Chef //
José Manuel Benito
Location //
Arrocería La Valenciana,
Valencia

PAELLA VALENCIANA
Chicken & rabbit paella

Serves 4

Preparation & cooking time
1hr & 30min

Recommended pan size: 42–46cm
  (16.5–18in) diameter
120ml (4 fl oz) olive oil
500g (17½oz), chicken, chopped into
  2½cm/1in chunks
500g (17½oz) rabbit, chopped into
  2½cm/1in chunks
200g (7oz) flat green beans, chopped
150g (5¼oz) garrofón beans (or butter
  beans), cooked & peeled
2 ripe, medium tomatoes, peeled &
  grated
pinch of salt, plus extra for seasoning
1 tsp mild smoked paprika
1½–2L (2¾–3½pt) chicken or
  vegetable stock
a few saffron threads
a sprig of fresh rosemary
250g (8¾oz) pre-cooked snails
  (optional)
400g (14oz) bomba rice (or short-
  grain rice)
salt & pepper, to taste
1 lemon, quartered, to serve

1 Put the paella pan over a low heat and heat the oil.

2 Once the oil is hot, keep the temperature low, and add the chicken pieces. Cook gently until they have browned all over, and move to the side of the pan. Add the rabbit pieces, brown them, then move to the side of the pan.

3 Put the green beans in the centre of the pan and fry, stirring to ensure they don't stick to the bottom of the pan. Then add the *garrofón* beans (or butter beans).

4 When cooked, move the beans to the side, and pour the grated tomato into the centre along with a pinch of salt. Stir with a wooden spoon until the tomato is cooked, then add the paprika, and mix all the ingredients together in the pan and stir thoroughly.

5 Fill the pan with the stock, which should almost reach the rim, and bring to the boil.

6 Add the saffron, the sprig of rosemary, and season to taste. Remove the rosemary sprig after 10 minutes and discard. Cook for approximately 30–40 minutes.

7 Keep an eye on the stock level: should it fall below the level of the paella pan's handles, add more water. Then add the cooked snails if using.

8 Pour the rice in a circular motion around the diameter of the pan.

9 Use a spatula to ensure that that the meat, vegetables and rice are mixed evenly together, but then refrain from stirring.

10 Return the mixture to the boil, and cook over a reasonably high heat for about 5 minutes, then at medium (or lower) heat for another 6 or 7 minutes or so, and finally over a low heat for another 6 or 7 minutes. (Total cooking time should be around 18 to 20 minutes.) Do not exceed this, or you will overcook the rice.

11 Once the paella has finished, leave it to rest for about 15 minutes. If the grains of rice are still hard, cover the paella pan with newspaper or with cardboard lightly sprinkled with water. Season with salt and pepper, and serve with a lemon wedge.

Tip

If the paella is short of broth, lower the heat to the minimum, and cover the top of the pan with aluminium foil. This will mean less evaporation.

TUMBET
Vegetable casserole

A ferociously modern take on a traditional Mallorcan peasant dish of slow-cooked peppers, tomato and aubergine, from the kitchen of experimentalist and locavore Miquel Calent.

Mallorca's most famous dish is closely related to Catalunya's *samfaina*, Castilla-La Mancha's *pisto manchego* and Andalucía's *alboronía*, and bears a resemblance to the French ratatouille. All combine red peppers, tomatoes and, often, onion and courgette, slowly fried in olive oil to create a sweet, Mediterranean dish that can be served as an accompaniment to meat or simply on its own with a hunk of crusty bread.

The elements of a *tumbet* (also spelled *tombet*) are often arranged in layers, like a lasagne, and the name means 'turned over', from the method of cooking it in a mould and tipping it out before serving. Miquel Calent takes this layering one step further, creating a nouvelle cuisine artwork in which the different elements are balanced in tiny stacks and topped with a cloud of tomato foam. Such theatrics are unexpected in this unassuming little restaurant in the peaceful market town of Campos, in the centre of the island, but Miquel is also a fan of bringing straightforward peasant cooking back into the limelight.

'These days,' he says, '*tumbet* is served as a side-dish to meat or fish, but this used to be considered a meal in itself. The Mallorcan diet used to be largely vegetarian – people mostly lived inland, working the soil. Fish dishes were only found on the coast, and workers could only afford to visit the sea once a year, once the grain had been winnowed. We ate much more healthily in those days, and only ate what grew nearby. I try and achieve that in the restaurant; my family has three vegetable gardens and we grow what we can and look to local producers for the rest. This,' he says, holding aloft a red pepper, 'was picked this morning. That's what we should all be striving for.'

Chef //
Miquel Calent
Location //
Ca'n Calent, Campos

TUMBET
Vegetable casserole

Serves 6

Preparation & cooking time 1hr, not including making tomato foam

For the tomato foam
750g (1½lb) tomato skins, seeds & stems
1L (1¾pt) cold water
30g (1oz) butter

For the tumbet
550g (19oz) whole new potatoes
100 ml (3½ fl oz)olive oil for baking, plus extra for frying
salt & pepper, to taste
1kg (2¼lb) beef floquet (floquet is hard to find outside Mallorca, but alternatives include sirloin or fillet steak), cleaned & cubed.
4 cloves of garlic, peeled
4 bay leaves
1 aubergine (eggplant), finely diced
1 red pepper, finely diced
1 courgette (zucchini), cut into thin strips & dusted with wholewheat flour
12 quail egg yolks
750ml (1½pt) chicken stock
250ml (½pt) beef stock
2–3 tbsp tomato chutney
tomato foam (see above)
salt & pepper, to taste

Tip

If you can get hold of the ingredients, professional chefs make tomato foam by adding 5g (¼oz) of soy lecithin and 20g (¾oz) of sucrose ester (sucro) to the tomato infusion instead of butter. (Note that both ingredients are added cold.)

For the tomato foam

1 In a pan, bring the tomatoes and the water up to 65°C (150°F), cook for five minutes and then remove from the heat. Leave overnight, and then strain into a bowl.

2 Heat the butter in a pan to 70°C (160°F), add to the tomato infusion, and beat with a hand-mixer to make the foam.

For the tumbet

1 Bake the potatoes in the oven for 20 minutes on a baking sheet/tray with a generous glug of olive oil drizzled over. Then puree with the oil used to bake them (leaving the skin on), and season well.

2 Sauté the beef in a non-stick pan for a couple of minutes then set to one side.

3 Put the garlic cloves and the bay leaves into a pan of hot oil, and fry for about a minute to infuse the oil. Remove the garlic and bay leaves, turn down the heat to 85°C (185°F), and fry the aubergine and pepper for about 10 minutes or until caramelised.

4 Remove the vegetables, set them aside, and heat the same oil to 185°C (365°F). Fry the courgette strips in the hot oil.

5 In a saucepan, poach the quail yolks in the combined chicken and beef stock at approximately 80°C (175°F) for 4 minutes until pale but still soft to the touch.

6 To serve, arrange the meat and eggs on top of spoonfuls of potato puree. Place the cubes of pepper and aubergine around the plate and dot with tomato chutney. Top the meat with the fried courgette, and the eggs with the tomato foam. Season with salt and pepper, to taste.

ÀNEC AMB PERES
Duck with pears

Out in the Catalan countryside, you'll see as much goose and duck on a menu as you will chicken, and the preferred way to serve it is with fruit.

High in the Guilleries hills, with a breathtaking view over the Sau reservoir, Fussimanya combines all that is great about Catalan country restaurants – artisanal products, an old stone farmhouse with picture-perfect views, and authentic recipes, such as this duck with pears, a Catalan favourite.

'This house has been in our family for 300 years,' says Josep Viladecàs Pascual, who runs Fussimanya with his sister Meri. 'My father was born here. It became a restaurant in 1971, and soon afterwards they started making sausages and charcuterie for the restaurant, and this business grew and grew. These days we have a stall in the Vic market, and eight shops. We're in no hurry to expand too much, though; this is very much a family business.'

'I learnt from my mother,' says Meri, who does most of the cooking. 'I did study in Barcelona, but then I went to live in Thailand for six years, to set up an NGO there for young refugees from Myanmar. We would take them off the streets and teach them to cook, give them a profession. We opened a little Spanish restaurant in Mae Sot, and the locals loved it – tortilla, meatballs, all those things. We had to adapt, mind, so we'd make our meatballs a little spicy!'

'Now that I'm back I've had to reboot my palate. After six years in a place like that, you don't taste things in the same way, and the products – the squid, the prawns, the duck – have a different flavour over there, so I've had to readjust. There is so much new information to process that it can be hard to go back to the authentic recipes without being tempted to mess around with them. But duck with pears is duck with pears – you can't add chilli to it,' she laughs.

Chef //
Meri Viladecàs Pascual
Location //
Fussimanya; Ctra Parador

ÀNEC AMB PERES

Duck with pears

Serves 4–6

Preparation & cooking time 2hr

4 duck legs
4 duck wings
salt & pepper, to taste
approx 100ml (3½ fl oz) olive oil, for frying
2 medium onions, roughly chopped
cloves of 1 head of garlic, unpeeled; plus 2 cloves of
   garlic, peeled & finely chopped
2 bay leaves
300g (10½oz) wild mushrooms of a meaty variety
1 handful of parsley, finely chopped
100ml (3½ fl oz) white wine
200ml (7 fl oz) chicken stock
4 ripe tomatoes
4 pears (preferably Conference), peeled, cored
   & chopped
200ml (7 fl oz) water
200ml (7 fl oz) Moscatel wine

1 Season the duck legs and wings with salt and pepper.

2 Heat 3–4 tbsp of the olive oil in a large saucepan, and add the duck pieces. Brown the duck and then add the onion, the (unpeeled) garlic cloves and the bay leaves.

3 Put 2 tbsp of olive oil in a separate frying pan, and sauté the mushrooms with the two cloves of chopped garlic and parsley until soft.

4 Add the white wine and chicken stock to the duck, along with the tomatoes and the mushrooms.

5 Put a lid on the saucepan, lower the heat and simmer until the meat is tender (about 60–90 minutes).

6 Put the pears, water and Moscatel wine in a separate saucepan. Bring to the boil, and then simmer until the pears are cooked al dente (about 10 minutes). Remove the pears from the juice and set aside.

7 About 10 minutes before the duck is ready, add the pears.

Tip

This dish is greatly improved if allowed to rest for a few hours, or even eaten the following day.

ARRÒS A BANDA
Fish-infused rice

It started life as a humble dish for fishers, made with the leftover catch too ugly to sell, but in the kitchens of Batiste nowadays, it can be hard to keep up with demand.

It all began in 1965 with a waiter named Batiste Juan Torres, who saved enough money to open his own restaurant on the seafront at Santa Pola, just outside Alicante. It was such a success that his renown spread and people would drive for miles to eat his famous rice dishes (what the untutored would call paellas, but to the aficionados a 'paella' is, strictly speaking, a paella valenciana, see p53).

Batiste's pièce de résistance was the *arròs a banda*, and he was said to be the first to serve this in a restaurant setting. Originally this was food for fishers, effectively made with the leftovers of the day's catch, and it was only once it became a fixture on restaurant menus that the second course of separate fish and shellfish was added.

The name means 'rice apart' and refers to the two servings; first the rice and second the seafood, although many just serve the fish-infused rice. The stock – used for both – is the all-important element, and is made up from *morralla*: a collective term for the fish considered too ugly or too bony to be served on the plate, but which makes for a tasty stock. Fish that work well for this are rascasse and monkfish, and whatever shellfish, such as shrimp and crab, that happen to be easily available.

David Baile Rodríguez, chef at Batiste, says they cook their version a little differently these days. 'We add squid and prawn to the rice. Strictly speaking, this is *arròs de senyoret*, with the shellfish peeled.' *Senyoret* means 'little nobleman', or someone who thinks themselves rather grand – rather too grand to shuck their own prawns. 'I've worked here since 1985,' David says, 'and in that time it [the dish] has developed in response to the demand of our customers, and these days it makes up 60% of our orders.'

Chef //
David Baile Rodríguez
Location //
Restaurante Batiste,
Santa Pola

ARRÒS A BANDA
Fish-infused rice

Serves 4

Preparation & cooking time 1hr 30min

9 tbsp olive oil
6 ñora peppers (or other dried red peppers)
cloves of 1 head of garlic, peeled & chopped
200g (7oz) ripe tomatoes, blended & strained
1kg (2¼lb) fish suitable for stock (monkfish &
    scorpion fish are especially good)
3L (5¼pt) water
600g (1¼lb) medium-grain rice
salt, to taste
6 saffron stamens
200g (7oz) fresh squid, chopped
2 prawns, peeled & chopped
1 red or green pepper, finely chopped & fried

1 Heat 3 tbsp of the olive oil in a small frying pan. Add the ñora peppers, and cook them gently for a few minutes.

2 Toast the garlic in 3tbsp of olive oil in a large saucepan. Add the tomatoes and stir.

3 Pour half of the garlic and tomato mix in a bowl to one side. To the remaining garlic-tomato mix, add the fish and the water to make the fish stock. Put the lid on and simmer for at least 40 minutes. Strain the liquid into a bowl, discarding the fish.

4 Put 3 tbsp of olive oil in a paella pan, and add the rice, salt, the saffron and the other half of the tomato and garlic mix reserved in a bowl. Fry for two minutes, stirring thoroughly to ensure that every grain is covered in the oil. Add the squid and the prawns, and sauté for another 2 or 3 minutes.

5 Add the hot fish stock to the paella pan and cook over a medium-high heat for 8 or 9 minutes. Add the chunks of fried pepper, and then lower the heat and cook for another 8 or 9 minutes, until the rice has absorbed all the fish stock.

6 Serve warm with *alioli* (p264).

Tip

When making the fish stock, be sure to clean the fish well and to remove all the viscera before cooking. When the stock has cooked, strain through a fine-meshed Chinois sieve.

COCHINILLO CON TUMBET

Roast suckling pig with tumbet

The Mallorcan cerdo negro is said to yield the most nutritious pork of any of its piggy relatives, and its number one ambassador is rising culinary star Andreu Genestra.

Although the idea of wresting recipes from the hands of grandmothers and turning them into something suitable for the 21st century has become deeply fashionable in Spain in recent years, there is a smaller and perhaps more significant movement afoot – that of resuscitating heritage breeds and heirloom crops. This partly reflects a resurgence of interest in eating organically and healthily, but in the case of Mallorca, which is at the vanguard of this trend, it has much to do with a sense of place and tradition.

'The black pig has been around for centuries in Mallorca,' says Andreu Genestra, chef at Aromata. 'It's bigger than the Iberian pig and its diet is different – it eats only figs, acorns, carob, legumes and grass – which changes the taste. When white pigs arrived in Mallorca in the '50s and '60s, farmers largely stopped breeding black pigs, since they have a smaller yield because of the higher fat content. What they didn't realise is how much they were losing in taste, and also that having less fat does not necessarily mean more nutritious.'

'These days they're bringing the black pig back because of the quality of its meat and its pedigree, but also because it's an animal that deals well with the Mallorcan climate. I come from a family of butchers, so I've had a lot of first-hand experience with all this. I can still remember the *matanzas* (traditional village pig slaughter) in winter, and the whole culture around that – the sausage-making, the families, the smells. I try and reflect all of that in my kitchen now, in the way I present this dish to my customers and in its aromas and flavours. The idea is to reflect those times and understand a little of the importance and culture surrounding the black pig, and how significant a part of life it has been for us.'

Chef //
Andreu Genestra
Location //
Aromata, Palma

COCHINILLO CON TUMBET
Roast suckling pig with tumbet

Serves 6

Preparation & cooking time 5hr, not including marinading/chilling time

1 oven-ready suckling pig (4½–5kg/10–11lb)
olive oil, for frying

For the marinade
juice of 1 orange
juice of 1 lemon
2 bay leaves
400ml (14 fl oz) chicken stock
200ml (7 fl oz) brandy
2 tsp salt
a pinch of white pepper
1 tsp pimentón dulce (sweet paprika)
2 cloves of garlic, chopped

For the seasoning
25g (1oz) tomato puree
juice & zest of one lime
1 tsp chopped fresh coriander
pinch of powdered garlic

For the tumbet
1kg (2lb) potatoes, peeled and sliced into rounds
olive oil, for frying
500g (1lb) aubergine (eggplant), peeled & sliced into rounds
500g (1lb) red pepper, finely chopped
750g (1lb 8oz) tomate frito (see p264)

1 Make the marinade by mixing together the orange, lemon, bay leaves, chicken stock, brandy, salt, pepper, paprika, chopped garlic cloves, and marinade the suckling pig for 6 hours.

2 Put the suckling pig on an oven tray, cover with foil, and cook at 135°C (275°F) for 4 hours and 30 minutes.

3 Leave to cool. Reserve the juice from the meat, and put the suckling pig skin to one side, taking care not to break it. Remove all the meat from the suckling pig.

4 To make the seasoning, mix together the tomato puree, lime, coriander and garlic with the reserved meat juice. Combine this with the meat, then press the meat between two baking trays to make a terrine, and leave to chill for 12 hours.

5 Cut the terrine into rectangles, and then fry in olive oil in a non-stick frying pan until golden (about 3 minutes) and put to one side.

6 Cut the large piece of pig skin into rectangles then, in a frying pan, lay one rectangle of pig skin between two sheets of greaseproof paper (to prevent sticking), and put a weight on it. Remove when golden. Repeat with all the rectangles.

7 To make the *tumbet*, gently fry the potato rounds in olive oil and set aside. Then do the same with the aubergine (eggplant) slices, and then the chopped peppers. Make a terrine by layering the potato, pepper and aubergine slices with the *tomate frito*. Put a weight on top of the terrine and leave to chill for 12 hours.

8 To serve, place a rectangle of crisped skin on top of a slice of the meat terrine. Add a slice of the *tumbet* terrine, and drizzle with the *tomate frito*.

ENSAÏMADA
Mallorcan pastries

Palma's Fornet de la Soca bakery creates beautifully moist and fragrant versions of the traditional lard pastry, using abundant olive oil and a centuries-old method.

There are many theories and legends around the origins of these sugar-dusted spiral pastries, and indications that something similar existed during various different occupations of the island, particularly during the Moorish invasion. Some say the shape imitates the turban that was worn at the time, and many sources state that the name comes from *saïm*, the Arabic word for lard, although that they would create and name a delicacy based on a foodstuff prohibited in the Koran seems unlikely.

For similar reasons, the oft-quoted tale that the Jewish community presented *ensaïmadas* to King Jaume I in gratitude for his releasing them from Arab rule is also somewhat illogical, unless – as in this recipe – olive oil was used in place of lard. Wherever they came from, they remain Mallorca's number one export, and huge beribboned octagonal boxes are a frequent sight at Palma airport.

'I have so many childhood memories of *ensaïmadas*,' says baker Tomeu Arbona. 'It was always present at family gatherings, and there was a little neighbourhood shop where we would buy them for breakfast at weekends, though I could have eaten them every day. I remember eating them with a cup of hot chocolate while opening Christmas presents.'

'I also remember my aunts kneading the dough and telling us Mallorcan folk stories. That was a Mallorca that no longer exists, but in the bakery I try to bring a little of that back by using old recipes and natural, local ingredients. At the Fornet de la Soca we don't make ours in spirals, we plait them as they did hundreds of years ago, and this preserves the moist texture and the aroma. It's also a nod to the Arab and Jewish influences that are still so present in our cooking after many years and have shaped the way we live.'

Chef //
Tomeu Arbona
Location //
Fornet de la Soca, Palma

ENSAÏMADA
Mallorcan pastries

Serves 4 to make one large ensaïmada

Preparation & cooking time 1hr,
plus a total of 18hr for the dough to rise

50g (1¾oz) fresh yeast
1kg (2¼lb) strong flour
250ml (8¾ fl oz) water
4 organic eggs
300g (10½oz) sugar
100g (3½oz) lard
150ml (5¼ fl oz) olive oil
icing sugar, to serve

1 Add the yeast and 300g (10½oz) of the flour to the water, and mix thoroughly. Cover with a clean cloth, and leave for one hour until it has doubled in volume.

2 In a separate bowl, beat together the eggs, sugar and 30g (1oz) of lard, and then add the yeast mixture.

3 Mix well, adding the rest of the flour until the dough is soft and smooth. Leave to rest for half an hour.

4 Knead the dough vigorously, breaking off sections and then kneading them back into the mixture. Rub olive oil around the bowl so that the dough does not stick.

5 Make a ball of the dough, cover it with a cloth and leave to rest for about 5 hours.

6 Roll out the dough with a rolling pin on a large oiled table top, making it as thin as possible. It should be almost transparent.

7 Melt the remaining lard in a small saucepan and smear the entire surface of the dough with it. Then cut the dough into two sections and roll them into long 'ropes' with the lard-smeared side on the inside. Leave them to rest for half an hour.

8 Twist the two strips together and arrange the dough clockwise in a loose spiral shape in a baking tin, and set aside for 12 hours to rise.

9 Bake at 150ºC (300ºF) for 35 minutes, then remove and allow to cool.

10 Dust liberally with icing sugar and serve.

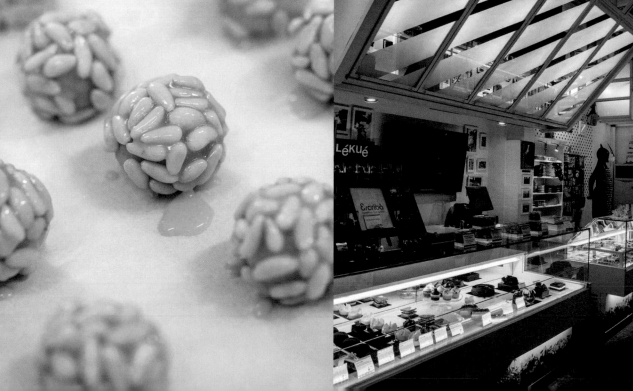

PANELLETS DE PINYONS
Marzipan balls with pine nuts

Dense balls of almond paste rolled in pine nuts are Catalunya's favourite Halloween treat. Playful pastry-chef and master chocolatier Christian Escribà reins in his maverick side to recreate a classic.

T raditionally eaten on and around All Saints' Day, the very Catalan custom of *panellets* (little buns) began over a century ago, when trays of this delicacy used to be raffled off in patisseries and cafes. As now, they were often made with potato, a cheaper and starchy alternative to the current almond-based confection, but master *pastisser* Christian Escribà has no time for such ersatz creations. 'You find unscrupulous people making them with potato but passing them off as made with almond and pricing them accordingly. And this idea that using potatoes keeps them moist, that's nonsense.'

Sourcing the almonds is also a careful business. 'I have a refiner – I buy the almonds whole and grind them myself. Why do you think ground almonds are cheaper than whole almonds? Because you've no idea what's in there, they can use old almonds, cheap almonds. It's like grated Parmesan or ground coffee, it's cheaper because they use a substandard ingredient.'

Of the fourth generation of a baking and chocolate-making dynasty (his father Antoni was known as the 'Mozart of chocolate'), Christian is nothing less than the Catalan Willy Wonka, a sculptor of chocolate, a lapidary of sugar. His Candy Glam rings were so sought after that they ended up in the jewellery sections of Harrods and Galeries Lafayette. But for all his alchemy, his respect for the finest raw materials is what sets him apart, something he thanks his parents for. 'My mother is French, and in a time when Spanish croissants were exclusively made with lard, she said to my father "Antoni, if you don't start using butter in croissants, I'm going back to France." And that's how my family came to produce the first butter croissants in Spain.'

'It's true,' he says, 'that you can make an edible *panellet* with sweet potato or potato, but for the real thing, it has to be almonds.'

Chef //
Christian Escribà
Location //
Escribà, Barcelona

PANELLETS DE PINYONS
Marzipan balls with pine nuts

Makes 35 balls

Preparation & cooking time 30min

250g (9oz) sugar
75ml (2½ fl oz) water
250g (9oz) ground Marcona almonds
2 (medium) eggs

For the coating
200g (7oz) pine nuts
1 beaten egg

1 Mix the sugar and water together, and boil until the mixture reaches 110°C (230°F); use a sugar (candy) thermometer to check the temperature is exact.

2 Remove the saucepan from the heat, and add the ground almonds.

3 Beat the eggs and gradually add them to the mix until a smooth and not too runny dough has formed, then leave to cool. If the dough needs thickening, add more ground almonds.

4 When the dough has cooled, roll the mixture into small balls of about 15g (½oz) or 2cm (¾in) in diameter.

5 Roll the balls first in beaten egg and then in pine nuts until completely covered.

6 Put the balls on a baking tray and brush carefully with beaten egg, ensuring that no pine nuts drop off.

7 Heat the oven to 300°C (570°F) and bake for 5 minutes. If your oven doesn't reach 300°C (570°F), then cook for longer at its highest temperature, eg for six minutes at 250°C (480°F). At such hot temperatures, you'll need to use two baking trays, stacked on top of each other to create a layer of air and ensure the *panellets* don't burn underneath.

PORTUGAL

SPAIN

Burgos

Palencia

14

VALLADOLID

Zamora

Castile-Leon

Soria

Salamanca

3

Segovia

15

Ávila

1

5

Guadalajara

MADRID ✦

7

16

9

13

8

Cuenca

4

Toledo

11

12

6

2

Cáceres

Trujillo

Guadalupe

**Castile-
La Mancha**

Extremadura

Badajoz

MÉRIDA

Ciudad Real

ALBACETE

SPAIN

10

Zafra

**Central
Spain**

CENTRAL SPAIN

Rich game dishes, the country's best cured ham, and slow, tender roasts in huge wood ovens dominate the cooking from the plains of central Spain, but not for nothing is landlocked Madrid known as 'Spain's greatest port' – the finest seafood arrives here every day in refrigerated trucks and takes pride of place in its restaurants.

PATATAS BRAVAS
Fried potatoes with spicy tomato sauce
page 82

SOPA DE TOMATE CON HIGOS
Tomato soup with figs
page 86

COCHINILLO
Suckling pig
page 90

PERDIZ ROJA CON HIERBAS SALVAJES Y ENEBRO
Red-legged partridge with wild herbs & juniper
page 94

BESUGO A LA MADRILEÑA
Madrid-style sea bream
page 100

PERDIZ ROJA CON ALMEJAS
Red partridge with clams
page 104

DOS TORTILLAS
Two tortillas: classic & deconstructed
page 108

BACALAO AL AJOARRIERO CON MANGO COULIS
Salt cod with garlic, potato & mango coulis
page 112

GALLINA EN PEPITORIA
Chicken with almonds, saffron & onions
page 116

REVUELTO DE SETAS
Scrambled eggs with wild mushrooms
page 120

LONCHEJAS DE CERDO IBÉRICO Y CALAMAR
Strips of pig's ear with squid
page 124

MIGAS EXTREMEÑAS
'Crumbs' from Extremadura
page 128

COCIDO MADRILEÑO
Madrid meat & chickpea stew
page 132

LECHAZO
Roast milk-fed lamb
page 136

YEMAS DE SANTA TERESA
Candied egg yolks
page 140

CHURROS
Fried dough sticks dusted in sugar
page 144

PATATAS BRAVAS

Fried potatoes with spicy tomato sauce

In the pantheon of Spain's subversive chefs, Paco Roncero is up there with the most revolutionary, but his take on everybody's favourite tapa is as respectful as it is playful.

The ubiquitous patatas brava is found in tapas bars from the Bay of Biscay to the Costa del Sol, with as many variations as there are regions. In their most basic form, these are diced fried potatoes, served with a tomato sauce. This should be spicy (hence the name – *brava* means wild, or fierce), but rarely is, at least to palates more accustomed to chilli than the Spanish. Some dispute the use of tomato at all, and insist that the colour should come from a generous quantity of *pimentón*, Spanish paprika.

In addition to the regional variations, there are probably more secret formulas for *brava* sauce than any other Spanish recipe, with myriad chefs creating their own unique version.

'It's very traditional, but it's an easy sauce on which to riff,' says chef Paco Roncero, the culinary mastermind behind Estado Puro, which takes classic tapas recipes and gives them a shake-up for the 21st century. 'There is any number of ways to give it a bit of a kick. These days people are adding Mexican chilli – we use cayenne – but these things come and go.'

Paco's own take on patatas bravas inverts the form, and the potato itself – a small new potato with the peel intact – becomes the receptacle for the piquant sauce. Crucially, the potatoes are fried in olive oil – to use vegetable oil would be to dishonour the dish – the insides partly scooped out to hold the salsa and a daub of *alioli* (p264), an emulsion of garlic and olive oil often confused with garlic mayonnaise but which doesn't contain eggs. *Alioli* is generally seen as Catalan, and not normally associated with *bravas* in Madrid. 'But it smooths off the spiciness,' says Paco. 'We have diners from all over the world, and everyone wants to try the *bravas*, but not all of them enjoy the heat. This version keeps everyone happy.'

Chef //
Paco Roncero
Location //
Estado Puro, Madrid

PATATAS BRAVAS
Fried potatoes with spicy tomato sauce

Serves 6

Preparation & cooking time 1hr

For the potatoes
800g (1¾lb) small new potatoes
approx. 500ml (17½ fl oz) olive oil for frying

For the salsa brava
160g (5½oz) onion, finely chopped
10g (½oz) pimentón dulce (sweet paprika)
a pinch of pimentón picante (spicy paprika)
4 small dried chillies
190g (6¾oz) plum tomatoes, peeled &
* finely chopped*
30ml (1 fl oz) sherry vinegar
1 tsp salt

1 Wash the potatoes in plenty of cold water, but leave the skins on.

2 Cut off a slice along the bottom of the potatoes so that they stand on a plate in a stable fashion.

3 Hollow out a small section of the middle of each potato with a teaspoon. This hollow will be filled with the *brava* sauce when you serve the potatoes.

4 Fry the potatoes in 3 tbsp of the olive oil in a large saucepan over a low heat until they are soft, then put aside.

5 To make the salsa brava, sauté the finely chopped onion in a large saucepan over a low heat until translucent, then add both kinds of paprika, the salt and the chillies, and continue to cook. Add the tomatoes, and allow to reduce over a low heat for about 30 minutes.

6 Add the vinegar to the mixture and cook for a further 15 minutes, blending to remove any lumps. Then bring to a boil, skimming off any foam if necessary, and set aside to settle at room temperature.

7 To prepare the dish, fry the potatoes in a deep-fryer (or high-sided, heavy-based saucepan) with the rest of the olive oil (or enough oil to cover the potatoes) at 180°C (350°F), until crisp.

8 Remove from the heat and fill the hollows in the warm potatoes with the salsa brava (now at room temperature) and some *alioli* (see recipe, p264).

SOPA DE TOMATE CON HIGOS
Tomato soup with figs

The stunning hilltop monastery of Guadalupe provides the setting for this no-nonsense restaurant, known for its warming tomato soup, served with figs (or grapes) amid the 16th-century Gothic cloisters.

Extremadura has conquistador Francisco Pizarro to thank for its vast tomato crop. More specifically, it has Pizarro's brutal subjugation of the Incas to thank – when he and his brothers returned to their Extremaduran homeland after conquering Peru, as well as tomatoes, they brought with them seeds for potatoes, peppers, avocados and cocoa, forever changing the way the Spanish, and eventually all Europeans, would eat.

But it's still tomatoes, more than any other crop, which have dramatically affected the fortunes of Pizarro's native region; Extremadura produces more than 90% of Spain's harvest. Despite being a remote, landlocked area, with freezing winters and roasting summers, it nonetheless has vast swathes of fertile valleys and pastureland, providing perfect growing conditions for sweet and flavourful vegetables.

'We've always had a glut of tomatoes in the region,' says Miguel Torrejón Álvarez, chef at the restaurant inside the 14th-century Guadalupe monastery. 'This dish was born out of that, as a way of using them up. And then we add figs, or grapes, depending what's in season. Lots of Spanish soups are served cold, but this one has always been hot. Years ago, the shepherds used to cook it over a fire and use it to warm themselves up.'

The monastery, partly run as a hotel, sits high on a hill in the Sierra de Villuercas. Its grandeur and the ecclesiastical treasures (including paintings by Francisco de Zurbarán, Francisco Goya and El Greco) contained within its walls attract a steady stream of visitors to this otherwise isolated spot. Since it opened its doors to the public, the monastery has been seen as having a culinary bent; it was a former monk who published the bestselling *100 recipes of Brother John of Guadalupe*. 'Since the beginning Guadalupe has been surrounded by orchards and vegetable gardens,' says Miguel. 'We're very lucky.'

Chef //
Miguel Torrejón Álvarez
Location //
Hospedería de Real
Monasterio, Guadalupe

SOPA DE TOMATE CON HIGOS

Tomato soup with figs

Serves 4

Preparation & cooking time 1hr

1 medium onion, chopped
1 large red pepper
2 large green peppers
4 cloves of garlic, chopped
2–3 tbsp olive oil
1kg (2¼lb) tomatoes, peeled
2 bay leaves
3 tbsp cumin
salt & pepper, to taste
1 tsp sugar (optional)
8 slices of day-old bread
figs, to serve (or grapes if figs are
not in season)

1 Blanch the tomatoes and skin them. Then finely chop all the vegetables.

2 Fry the onions and three of the chopped garlic cloves in the olive oil slowly over a low heat in a large saucepan. When they begin to brown, add the red and green peppers and cook until softened.

3 Add the peeled tomatoes and the bay leaves, and cook until all the juice has been released from the tomatoes.

4 Chop the remaining clove of garlic and add to the soup with the cumin.

5 Season to taste; if it's a touch acidic, add some sugar. Remove the bay leaves.

6 Arrange the slices of bread on the bottom of an earthenware dish, then pour over the piping hot soup and serve, accompanied by figs (or grapes, depending on the season).

COCHINILLO
Suckling pig

Iconic 19th-century restaurant Mesón de Cándido is revered all over Spain for its juicy suckling pig and the rituals that surround its roasting and solemn entrance into the lavish dining room.

Ask anyone in Spain to name the restaurant that best represents Castilla y León and chances are that the Mesón de Cándido will be the answer. Half-timbered and arcaded, its Dickensian front has almost as many tourist cameras pointed at it as the vast Roman aqueduct that looms above it, and the line of people that gathers at midday and dinner time is here for one thing and one thing only – succulent, sticky and tender roast suckling pig.

The restaurant has been going since 1884, presided over by a long line of Cándidos, one of which – Cándido López, father of the current incumbent – began the tradition of carving the meat with the edge of a plate as a demonstration of just how crisp the skin should be, and just how yielding the flesh within. This has now become something of a ceremony – along with a solemn proclamation as the piglet is brought into the dining room – and is now observed in *asadores* (roasting houses) all over Segovia.

'There are many key factors that influence the taste and texture of the pork,' says chef Alberto Cándido. 'The piglet should weigh between five and 5.3kg, usually when they are 15 or 20 days old. At this age their only food will have been milk, so the mother's diet is key – she should be fed on good quality cereals: barley, corn, wheat bran and soy flour.'

As to the roasting process, it's a slow one, so it's important not to let the meat dry out. 'The first thing to do is paint the skin with lard, which conducts the heat better than water. The outer layer is going to form a crust, which will stop the juices escaping and provide the perfect crunch, in contrast to the flesh inside, which will be soft and juicy.'

Chef //
Cándido López
Location //
Mesón de Cándido, Segovia

COCHINILLO
Suckling pig

Serves 6

Preparation & cooking time 2hr

1 cleaned suckling pig (approx 4½kg/10lb)
salt, to taste
several bay leaf stems
water
100g (3½oz) lard

1 Using a cleaver or a large knife, split the suckling pig in two lengthwise along the spine. Season with salt.

2 Arrange the bay leaf stems in an earthenware dish, and then place the suckling pig (skin-side down) on top, so that it doesn't touch the bottom of the dish. Pour over the water until it reaches a depth of about 1cm (⅓in).

3 Roast the pig in a pre-heated oven at 180°C (350°F) for one hour, then remove from the oven and turn, so that the skin side is facing upwards.

4 Prick the pig skin with a knife a few times to ensure air bubbles don't form, then apply the lard to the skin with a brush, and return to the oven. Cook for another 45 minutes or so, until the suckling pig is golden brown all over, and the skin is crunchy.

5 Serve the roast pig with the juices left from cooking, adjusting for seasoning, alongside it.

PERDIZ ROJA CON HIERBAS SALVAJES Y ENEBRO
Red-legged partridge with wild herbs & juniper

Adolfo is nothing short of an institution, a social hub for Toledo residents and a place that madrileños will drive to just for lunch. Locally caught game is where it excels.

'In terms of hunting,' says chef Adolfo Muñoz Martín, swinging his arms wide 'the most important region in all of Europe is Castilla-La Mancha. Toledo, Ciudad Real, Albacete, Cuenca, Guadalajara... all these areas [within Castilla-La Mancha] have a lot of woods and a lot of game. You'll find all kinds of deer, wild boar, turtle doves, partridge, wood pigeons, thrush, rabbits and hare; there's a huge number for every season of the year.'

The undisputed star of the Toledo kitchen, however, is the red partridge. Adolfo's signature dish is a different take on the stewed *toledano* classic, steaming the thighs and searing the breast on a hot plate (ubiquitous in Spanish kitchens, but a frying pan will do just as well). He then places them on a plate with a smear of deep-red onion sauce and a bright yellow quenelle of sweet potato, an artist's palette of colour, texture and taste, on which a pipette of the reduced stock rests, for the diners to add themselves.

These are unexpectedly modern touches in these venerable dining rooms, where blood-red walls hung with 15th-century oil paintings meet polychromatic coffered ceilings and ancient beams. The restaurant was once two buildings: one from the 9th century and the other from the 12th-century. A short walk away, the family has a wine cellar to rival any in Spain; 32,000 bottles from all over the world sitting in a carefully controlled brick-vaulted basement that dates back to the 9th century and contains Roman elements.

Within these hallowed spaces, and considering his respect for the classic recipes of old, Adolfo is not hidebound by tradition as one might expect. His obsession with eating healthily goes back a long way: 'I've always felt food should be prepared in the simplest way possible,' he says. 'Find alternatives to sugar, use less salt, and buy the very best olive oil you can. Your body will thank you for it.'

Chef //
Adolfo Muñoz Martín
Location //
Adolfo, Toledo

PERDIZ ROJA CON HIERBAS SALVAJES Y ENEBRO

Red-legged partridge with wild herbs & juniper

Serves 4

Preparation & cooking time 1hr

4 oven-ready partridges
3–4 tbsp olive oil, for frying
60g (2oz) wild mushrooms
sea salt, to serve
thyme leaves, to serve

For the marinade
100ml (3½ fl oz) chicken stock
1 head of garlic, cloves peeled
8 black peppercorns
4 juniper berries
pinch sea salt
4 sprigs of thyme
4 sprigs of oregano
4 sprigs of rosemary

For the sweet potato cream
1 roast sweet potato
100ml (3½ fl oz) chicken stock
salt & pepper, to taste

For the red onion cream
1 roast red onion
1 roast beetroot
salt & pepper, to taste

1 Using a very sharp knife, cut each partridge into four pieces (two legs and two breasts). Slice out the small tenderloin from each breast and reserve. (Also reserve the carcass for making stock.)

2 Prepare the marinade by putting the chicken stock, garlic cloves, peppercorns, juniper berries, a pinch of sea salt and the leaves from the sprigs of thyme, oregano and rosemary in a food processor and liquidise.

3 Put the partridge tenderloins in the marinade.

4 Seal the partridge legs in a vacuum bag, and cook sous-vide at a low temperature until tender (reserve the cooking juices for later). Alternatively, put a dash of olive oil in a frying pan and sauté the partridge legs until just golden, and then roast in a pre-heated oven at 180°C (350°F) for about 6–8 minutes.

5 Heat 2–3 tbsp of olive oil in a frying pan, and lightly brown the partridge breasts.

6 Make the sweet potato cream by liquidising the roast sweet potato in the chicken stock and adding salt and pepper to taste.

7 Make the red onion cream by liquidising the roasted onion and the beetroot, and seasoning to taste.

8 Sauté the wild mushrooms in a little olive oil.

9 Just before serving, remove the tenderloin from the marinade and fry briefly until just cooked.

10 Heat up the legs in the juice that was produced by cooking them sous-vide, if applicable. If you roasted the legs, heat them in some of the marinade. Then put the juices/marinade in a jug to serve with the dish.

11 To serve, put a swirl of the red onion cream on each plate, along with a quenelle of the sweet potato cream.

12 Lay the tenderloin on top of the cream, followed by the breast, and then the legs.

13 Arrange the wild mushrooms on each plate, sprinkle over some sea salt and thyme leaves.

BESUGO A LA MADRILEÑA

Madrid-style sea bream

After falling into disrepair, the ancient Taberna La Carmencita, which once hosted poet Neruda and playwright Lorca, has been lovingly restored, along with time-honoured recipes, like this succulent baked sea bream.

At 160 years old, Taberna La Carmencita is the second oldest restaurant in Madrid. It's been through some troubled times in recent decades, including a long period of closure and an ignominious stint as a pizza restaurant. In the hands of restaurateur Carlos Zamora, it has had its old-time charm restored, and a thoroughly modern philosophy – slow food, locally sourced, with an emphasis on organic and free-range produce – imposed in the kitchen.

The colourful wall tiles are gleaming anew, as is the ancient zinc bar and the bronze luggage racks above the tables. Mismatched porcelain is everywhere on display and the old ladies who come for a cheeky morning *vermut* (vermouth) sip it from elegant martini glasses. In one corner is the table where Pablo Neruda used to sit and write his poetry. Playwright Federico García Lorca once lived in the flat above, and would come down to the tavern to join the literati in late-night *tertulias* (artistic gatherings).

The menu speaks of happy chickens and line-caught fish, artisanal cheeses and wild herbs. Classic recipes have been brought to life, among them the *besugo a la madrileña*, a mighty beast that lies slathered in onion, tomato and garlic, on a bed of sliced potatoes.

'Although we have no port in Madrid,' says chef Salvador González Alcoholado, 'the *besugo* recipe dates back to the 19th century. It actually started out as a dish for the poor, but once it reached the ears of the nobility, it turned into a dish for royals.' The fish comes from the market in Santander, in a specially refrigerated van that makes the trip to the capital several times a week.

'For many years now,' says Salvador, 'this has been a dish for people of every class, and you'll find it in restaurants across Madrid. Its appeal is that it manages to be both simple and delicious at the same time.'

Chef //
Salvador González
Alcoholado
Location //
Taberna La
Carmencita, Madrid

BESUGO A LA MADRILEÑA
Madrid-style sea bream

Serves 4–6

Preparation & cooking time 1hr

2kg (4.4lb) sea bream, gutted & scaled
1 medium lemon, sliced
500g (1lb) peeled potatoes, cut into ½cm
* (¼in) slices*
4 plum tomatoes, cut into 1cm (½in) slices
400g (14oz) onion, finely chopped
1 head of garlic, cut in half
1 handful of chopped parsley
1 bay leaf
sea salt, to taste
white pepper, to taste
150ml (5½ fl oz) oil
150ml (5½ fl oz) fish stock
250ml (9 fl oz) good quality white wine

1 Preheat the oven to 200°C (390°F).

2 Make four diagonal slits in one side of each sea bream, and place the lemon in the slits.

3 Put the potato, tomato and onion in a fish kettle (or large baking dish), then add the garlic, parsley, bay leaf and sea bream. Pour over the olive oil and season to taste.

4 Put the kettle in the pre-heated oven and, after 5 minutes, lower the temperature to 175°C (350°F) and cook for a further 25 minutes. If your bream is much smaller (or you're using two small ones), reduce the cooking time for the fish from 40 minutes to 20–30 minutes.

5 Add the fish stock and the wine to the fish kettle, and cook for another 15 minutes. Serve piping hot.

Tip

It's important to check on the bream after 30 minutes; if the fish is ready but the potatoes are not, cover with foil and continue cooking until the potatoes are tender. Or remove the bream, wrap it in foil and keep it warm. The bream is cooked when the whites of the eyes turn white.

PERDIZ ROJA DE CAMPO, ESTOFADO AL VINO BLANCO CON ALMEJAS

Partridge stewed with white wine & clams

The stunning town of Trujillo is often used for film sets, its medieval heart barely touched over time. It's also home to some great restaurants, where game is held in the highest regard.

Driving around Spain, many outsiders are baffled by the numerous '*coto de caza*' signs demarcating fenced-off (or even apparently open) tracts of land. These are 'game reserves', where – for several months of the year – shooting parties roam through the bush. Every type of game is hunted here, from deer to wild boar, but partridge is perhaps the most prevalent. The importance of the *perdiz* (red-legged partridge, to be precise) is summed up in the Spanish saying '*Fueron felices y comieron perdices*' – 'They were happy and they ate partridges'. Which is essentially a way of saying 'They lived happily ever after'.

'You cook a partridge in many ways,' says Antonio Sánchez, owner and chef at the Corral del Rey restaurant. 'Some people make it with chocolate, or with onions and carrots. This recipe, with clams, is a personal favourite. It's a little bit different, but the flavours are intense. You might point out that we're miles from the sea, but in Spain we say that the best sea port we have is Madrid. Madrid is nowhere near the coast, but that's where all the best seafood goes, and that's where we get ours. Everything else is local.'

In the remote Trujillo, it needs to be. But it is exactly its isolation that makes it so unspoilt and charming. One of the most beautiful towns in Spain, it has an astounding array of baroque and Renaissance palaces that reflect its heritage as the birthplace of some of the most successful 16th-century conquistadores, and the wealth generated from their endeavours. At its heart is the splendid Plaza Mayor, where the Corral del Rey takes up a former annexe of the 16th-century Palacio de Piedras Albas. 'We've had a few difficult years with the recession,' says Antonio. 'But it's picking up. In a town this pretty people will always come back.'

Chef //
Antonio Sánchez Garcia
Location //
Corral del Rey, Trujillo

PERDIZ ROJA DE CAMPO, ESTOFADO AL VINO BLANCO CON ALMEJAS

Partridge stewed with white wine & clams

Serves 4

Preparation & cooking time 1hr

4 oven-ready partridges
salt & ground white pepper, to taste
100ml (3½ fl oz) olive oil
2 onions, finely diced
4 cloves of garlic, chopped
2 bay leaves
1 sprig of thyme
1 tsp black peppercorns
125ml (4½ fl oz) dry white wine
500ml (17½ fl oz) chicken stock (or water)
16 clams

1 Season the partridges with salt and white pepper.

2 Heat the olive oil in a large saucepan and cook the partridges until the skin is golden. Remove them from the pan, and set aside.

3 Add the onion, garlic, bay leaves, thyme (leaves only) and black peppercorns to the olive oil, and fry gently over a low heat.

4 Put the partridges back in the saucepan, and pour over the wine. Simmer for about 10–15 minutes, or until the wine has reduced.

5 Add the chicken stock or water, and simmer for another 10–15 minutes.

6 Wash the clams thoroughly, and put them in a separate pan. Add around 1cm (½in) of water, put a lid on the saucepan, and bring to the boil. The clams should steam open in 2 or 3 minutes. Remove the clams and set aside.

7 Add the water used to open the clams to the stew and simmer for 5 minutes.

8 Adjust the seasoning to taste. Serve the partridge with the wine sauce and scatter over the clams.

DOS TORTILLAS

*Two tortillas: classic &
deconstructed*

*Puckish chef
Nino Redruello
plays with the
time-honoured
tortilla to make
a deconstructed
version so rich
and flavoursome
that the most
reactionary of
critics would
struggle to
find fault.*

The Non-Authentic Caesar Salad, Infiltrated Chicken Wings, Pedigree Hot Dog – just some of the subversive snacks dotting the menu of La Gabinoteca. Santiago Redruello, who founded this Madrid restaurant dynasty when he opened La Estrecha in 1930, would be turning in his grave. His grandson Nino, dressed in denim shirt and Apple watch, grins. 'We like these games. When people come in we give them a wine list in the form of a flow chart, and they have to answer questions about themselves – Beatles or Stones? Paragliding or surfing the net? Wagner or Mozart? – and this will lead them to their ideal wine. It's fun. But, obviously, if everything is a game it gets boring. This is why we have a series of "wow" dishes – usually based on historic comfort food done with a twist – then we mix them in with serious, traditional ones that are all about flavour.'

Which brings us to the tortilla. The first, the tortilla *velazqueña*, is named for the street (Calle Velázquez) where the first family restaurant opened, but is essentially a classic tortilla, following an age-old recipe. Little tweaks of Nino's devising make it extra juicy, with a pleasing contrast of crunch and softness, but this is a version with which his grandfather would be familiar.

The *potito*, meanwhile, is named after jars of baby food, but was also inspired by Nino's fascination for the way people preserve food in the countryside, and how these '*conservas*' have now become fashionable in gourmet shops and bars. It is served in little screw-top jars warmed in a bain-marie, and contains layers of creamy potato puree, crunchy fried potatoes, a barely poached egg and a final umami hit of truffle, and is designed to be eaten by plunging the spoon to the bottom and catching a scoop of everything on the way back up.

Chef //
Nino Redruello
Location //
La Gabinoteca, Madrid

DOS TORTILLAS
Two tortillas: classic & deconstructed

Tortilla velazqueña serves 2
El potito serves 4

Preparation & cooking time
Tortilla velazqueña 30min
El potito 1hr

For the tortilla velazqueña/classic tortilla
250g (9oz) potatoes (ideally Mona Lisa or
*   Quebec)*
approx. 4 tbsp olive oil, for frying
½ onion, chopped finely
2 free-range eggs and one egg yolk

For the potito/deconstructed tortilla
150g (5½oz) floury potatoes for mashing,
*   unpeeled*
a quarter of a leek, chopped
200ml (7 fl oz) milk
a generous knob of butter
salt & pepper, to taste
150g (5½oz) potatoes (Mona Lisa or other
*   waxy ones) for frying, unpeeled*
100ml (3½ fl oz) olive oil
salt & pepper, to taste
4 medium free-range eggs
8g (⅓oz) black truffle (Tuber
*   melanosporum)*
2 tsp truffle oil
4 small jars with lids for serving

For the tortilla *velazqueña*/classic tortilla

1 Peel the potatoes, slice them thinly and chop into pieces.

2 Fry about three quarters of the potato slices gently in olive oil over medium heat (150°C/300°F) until they are cooked through, but aren't crisp. Fry the remainder in hot oil until they are crisp.

3 Sauté the chopped onion in a pan over a medium-low heat until caramelised.

4 Mix all the potato with the onion, and add the eggs and the egg yolk.

5 Heat a little more oil in a cast iron frying pan to ensure the tortilla doesn't stick, and add the egg and potato mixture. Cook over a medium heat until the outside is cooked, and the inside remains runny. Turn out and serve.

For the *potito*/deconstructed tortilla

1 In a saucepan, cover the floury potatoes and the leek with water and bring to the boil. Then strain off the water, and boil for another 10 minutes with the milk and butter. Season with salt and pepper. Blend to form a smooth cream.

2 Peel the frying potatoes and slice finely (the slices should be about 1mm to 2mm thick). Fry them slowly at 120°C (250°F) in the olive oil in a pan until they are soft, then raise temperature to 200°C (390°F) to make them crisp and golden. Season with salt and pepper.

3 Put the cream of potato and leek at the bottom of each jar, then add slices of fried potato, and crack open the egg on top. Season, grate over the truffle and add a swirl of truffle oil.

4 Put the lids on the jars, and cover with water in a bain-marie (or a saucepan with a cloth at the bottom), and cook slowly for 20 minutes or until set. Remove the jars, dry them off, and serve them closed.

Tip

The extra egg yolk in the tortilla velazqueña makes it creamier, and frying the potatoes
in two batches at different heat makes for a more interesting texture.
When serving the potito, make sure that the potato cream is not too runny, as the egg serves to make the combination
more liquid when cooked. Cook it at the lowest heat possible to preserve the creaminess of the egg white.

BACALAO AL AJOARRIERO CON MANGO COULIS

*Salt cod with garlic,
potato & mango coulis*

*Creamy, garlicky
ajoarriero is found
in restaurants
across central and
northern Spain,
but here it comes
in tandem with
a dramatic view
from the terrace at
Figón del Huécar.*

It's an imposing sight: Cuenca's *casas colgadas* (hanging houses) rise out of the bedrock at the top of a steep gorge at the confluence of the rivers Huécar and Júcar. Already teetering at a vertiginous height, some of these buildings rise a further eight storeys, with wooden balconies jutting out over the ravine in a truly hair-raising manner. The terrace at Figón del Huecar shares this spectacular view, but sits on more solid ground.

Opened as a restaurant in 2004, it was for 20 years the home of successful Spanish singer José Luis Perales, and draws a mix of inquisitive fans and gourmands. One of its most popular dishes is the *bacalao al ajoarriero*, a dish with a curious history. It was born out of the *trashumancia*, the centuries-old system of grazing migration routes that shepherds and others use to move their flocks to wherever the grass is, literally, greener. These same routes were used by mule-drivers (*arrieros*, from which the dish takes its name), who would transport provisions and foodstuffs from town to town. One such ingredient was dried salted cod, still widely used in Spain, and which would easily weather the journey from the coast.

'It's a dish that captures history as well as the essence of the place,' says chef Ángel Gómez Caballero. 'As well as produce from the sea, the muleteers would pick up vegetables and so on along the way. It might be garlic, potatoes, oil or eggs, depending on the route and the place.' This may explain why *ajoarriero* is popular in so many parts of Spain and takes so many different forms.

'Even within Cuenca it has its own variations, but the one that we make is particularly subtle in flavour – we try and balance all the ingredients so nothing is too intrusive, and creates a harmonious whole.'

Chef //
Ángel Gómez Caballero
Location //
Figón del Huécar, Cuenca

BACALAO AL AJOARRIERO
CON MANGO COULIS

Salt cod with garlic, potato & mango coulis

Serves 4

***Preparation & cooking time 30min, not
including soaking the salted cod/chilling time***

1kg (2¼lb) potatoes, peeled and cut into chunks
400g (14oz) salt cod (soaked for 24 hours)
2 cloves of garlic, crushed
1 egg plus 1 egg yolk
100g (3½oz) breadcrumbs
500ml (1pt) sunflower oil
salt, to taste
1 mango, peeled & roughly chopped
50g (1¾oz) sugar
125ml (4½ fl oz) water
2 boiled eggs, chopped, to serve
handful of parsley, finely chopped
4 slices toasted bread

1 Soak the salt cod for 24 hours to remove the salt, changing the water three or four times before rinsing with cold water at the end.

2 Peel and cut the potatoes into chunks. Add the cod, cover with water, and boil for 20 minutes.

3 Strain off the water, then mash the potatoes and cod together, and leave to chill for 12 hours.

4 Gently whisk together the garlic, the raw egg and the egg yolk.

5 Add the potato and cod, and then the breadcrumbs, and continue to mix.

6 Add the sunflower oil very slowly while whisking continuously. Add salt to taste.

7 Make a coulis by blending the mango chunks with the sugar and the water.

8 To serve, put the *ajoarriero* in the centre of a plate, top with the chopped boiled eggs and the parsley, and decorate with the mango coulis and the toasted bread.

GALLINA EN PEPITORIA
Chicken with almonds, saffron & onions

A storied but thoroughly unpretentious restaurant that has changed little in decades, Casa Ciriaco has served its famous chicken en pepitoria to artists, bullfighters, actors and royalty.

Originally a humble peasant dish, possibly with its roots in Arabian cooking, *Gallina en pepitoria* was given a royal boost when Isabella II – a frequent visitor to the Casa Ciriaco – made it a favourite at the turn of the 19th century. Isabella II was known as 'Spain's nymphomaniac queen', and knew a thing or two about the good life, and it's probably thanks to her patronage that this quintessentially Madrid *taberna* became as successful as it did, and continues so to this day.

If these walls could talk, they would tell tales not only of the regal Bourbon hedonist, along with the various writers, artists, bullfighters and politicians who for years treated Casa Ciriaco as a second home – and whose photos and heartfelt scribbles still adorn the walls, but also of the tragic attack on the wedding parade of Alfonso XIII and Victoria Eugenia in 1906. A disgruntled anarchist threw a bomb hidden in a bouquet of flowers from a balcony above the restaurant, and 23 people were killed on its doorstep.

It was a few years after that Ciriaco Muñoz took the reins, which were handed down to his niece Amparo in 1967. 'I've been making this dish for nearly 50 years,' she says, 'using the same century-old recipe. Why would I change it? Other versions can be good, but for me, for example, it has to be *gallina*, not *pollo*. *Gallina* is fundamental to the *pepitoria*.' Aromatic, creamy and rich, Ciriaco's take is still considered the definitive Madrid dish, and the kitchen turns out over 40 helpings a day.

'They have a saying in Spain,' says Amparo. *'Con gallina en pepitoria, bien se puede ganar la Gloria.'* With chicken in pepitoria, you can go to Heaven.

Chef //
Amparo Moreno
Location //
Casa Ciriaco, Madrid

GALLINA EN PEPITORIA
Chicken with almonds, saffron & onions

Serves 2

Preparation & cooking time 3–4hr

1 gallina (older hen – see boxed text)
salt
approx. 4 tbsp olive oil for frying
250ml (8½ fl oz) water
250ml (8½ fl oz) white wine
6 cloves of garlic, chopped
a handful of fresh parsley, chopped
two bay leaves
75g (2½oz) ground almonds
25g (1oz) breadcrumbs
large pinch of saffron
1 onion, finely chopped
50g (2oz) flour

1 Cut the chicken into large pieces and sprinkle with salt. Sauté for a couple of minutes in olive oil until the pieces begin to brown.

2 Bring the water to the boil in a large, deep, heavy-bottomed saucepan (or cast-iron casserole dish), and add the white wine, the garlic, the parsley, and the bay leaves.

3 Mix together the ground almonds, breadcrumbs, and a pinch of salt and saffron, and add to the saucepan mixture.

4 Add the chicken pieces, and cook over a medium heat for 2½ hours.

5 In a separate pan, fry the onion over a low heat until translucent, then add the flour, and cook for a few minutes.

6 Add the onion to the stew and simmer until the sauce has thickened and the chicken is tender.

Gallina or pollo?

Spanish chefs distinguish between pollo – a young chicken bred for its meat, and generally killed after six weeks – and gallina, an older hen, normally free-range and often one that has been used to lay eggs. The meat is darker and slightly tougher, but adds much better flavour in stews and slow-cooked food.

REVUELTO DE SETAS

Scrambled eggs with wild mushrooms

Unspoilt, picturesque Zafra is one of Extremadura's prettiest towns, and its diminutive size belies the spread of superb eating options. José Luís Entradas is a quiet champion of the region's food.

Few dishes are as widely eaten across the globe as scrambled eggs. In South America they're spicy, in Morocco they are sour, in the UK they're unlikely to be meddled with much beyond the occasion addition of smoked salmon. Mostly they are known as a breakfast food, but in Spain they have a thousand uses. Their smooth flavour makes them the perfect vehicle for the first asparagus shoots in spring, or for tiny shrimp, or – in autumn – wild mushrooms.

Foraging for wild mushrooms is a national sport in Spain, particularly in the north of the country but also in Extremadura, close to the Portuguese border. The inventiveness of the dishes created around them is glorious, with high-end restaurants competing for how many varieties and how many methods of preparing them can appear on one plate. José Luis Entradas de Barco prefers to keep it simple.

'This is why eggs are ideal,' he says. 'What I love about this dish is that it showcases everything I love about Extremaduran produce. Wild mushrooms are such an important element of autumn food here, and if you can get cured Extremadura ham, it's perfect with eggs. I also add a little bit of Torta La Serena cheese, which is a pungent, creamy sheep's cheese, also from Extremadura, though you could easily substitute for something with a similar texture and taste.'

'Anyone can make this dish, of course, but there is a little trick to doing it well. You have to cook the eggs on the lowest heat possible. Heat the pan, then remove it from the flame and let the eggs cook on the heat of the pan, stirring all the while. Put it back, take it off, as many times as you need to. It takes a little patience, but it's worth it.'

Chef //
José Luís Entradas del Barco
Location //
La Rebotica, Zafra

REVUELTO DE SETAS
Scrambled eggs with wild mushrooms

Serves 4

Preparation & cooking time 30min

2–3 tbsp extra virgin olive oil
½ leek, finely chopped
500g (1lb) Amanitas Caesareas (Caesar's
*   mushrooms), boletus/cep or similarly meaty*
*   wild mushrooms, finely chopped*
salt & black pepper, to taste
4 beaten eggs
4 slices of cured Iberian ham
1 tbsp Torta La Serena cheese (or other creamy
*   sheep's cheese)*
30ml (1 fl oz) truffle oil

1 Put 2–3 tbsp of the olive oil in a frying pan, and fry the chopped leek and mushrooms gently over a low heat.

2 When the mixture is cooked, season with salt and pepper and add the (very loosely beaten) eggs.

3 Turn the heat down to low, and stir continuously. Remove from the heat just before the eggs become solid, to retain some of the juice.

4 Top the scrambled eggs with the slices of ham and the cheese, and drizzle with black truffle oil.

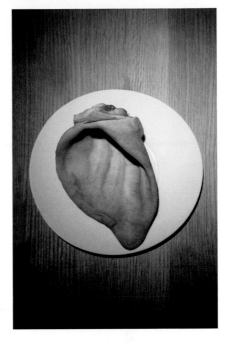

LONCHEJAS DE CERDO IBÉRICO Y CALAMAR

Strips of pig's ear with squid

A quintessentially Spanish ingredient, the pig's ear is given an unexpectedly ludic oriental makeover at Atrio, the luxurious Cáceres hideaway of garlanded chef Toño Pérez.

Listening to Toño Pérez talk about pigs' ears is quite a revelation. 'The texture of the cartilage of the ear, the consistency of it and the slightly gelatinous flavour, is very similar to the texture of squid, if you cook it a certain way. The ear is cooked on a grill, and has that carbon taste as though it had been cooked over a fire in the country. The sauce is reduced and slightly sticky, like the meat, and that brings the elements together and brings some harmony to the dish.'

Harmony is important to Toño, and everything in his restaurant and hotel, a luxurious Relais & Châteaux boutique, is carefully measured to bring out the original architectural elements while creating light-filled spaces that are entirely 21st century. From the outside, the building blends in perfectly with the picture-postcard honey-coloured medieval ensemble of buildings that forms Cáceres' old town, while the interiors dazzle with virtuoso artworks and modern lines. The wine cellar in itself is a feat of bleeding-edge engineering, as it needs to be to house one of the world's great wine collections, including an assiduously cared-for Château d'Yquem from 1806 (retailing for a cool €310,000).

His cooking shows this same preoccupation with respecting the old while welcoming the new. 'This combination of elements from the land and from the sea is typical of Extremadura and the neighbouring Alentejo, to the west in Portugal. It might seem strange, given that we're landlocked, but we're only a couple of hours from the Portuguese coast.' The dish's Asian feel stems from Toño's love of the food from that region, and he's made many trips to Thailand, in particular. 'It's an easy dish to make – quick, simple, no special skills required – but it's playful. It's completely *extremeño* and completely Asian at the same time. It's fun.'

Chef //
Toño Pérez
Location //
Atrio Restaurante
Hotel, Cáceres

LONCHEJAS DE CERDO IBÉRICO Y CALAMAR

Strips of pig's ear with squid

Serves 6

Preparation & cooking time 3½hr, including freezing squid

100g (3½ oz) squid body
1 Iberian pig's ear
1 onion studded with 4 cloves
2 bay leaves
2 tsp peppercorns
a sprig of rosemary
2 tsp salt
600ml (1pt) water
100ml (3½ fl oz) soy sauce
2 tsp Modena balsamic vinegar
2 rounded tsp cornflour
50ml (1¾ fl oz) oloroso or other sweet sherry
salt & pepper, to taste
3 leaves pak choi, finely chopped
½ Granny Smith apple (or other tart apple for
    cooking, if out of season)
olive oil for frying
a handful of mustard sprouts (or alfafa sprouts)
1 heaped tsp Madras curry powder
marigold flowers (or other edible flowers), to serve

1 Skin the squid, score the body and tenderise (see Tip).

2 Put the pig's ear, the onion with the cloves, the bay leaves, peppercorns, rosemary, salt and water in a saucepan. Cook for about 40 minutes until the ear is tender. Drain 500ml (17½ fl oz) of the stock into a saucepan and put the ear aside for later.

3 Take the saucepan of the pig's ear stock and reduce it by simmering over a medium heat with the soy sauce and balsamic vinegar. Mix the cornflour with the sherry and then add to the stock. Thicken until the sauce turns glossy, then season to taste.

4 Sauté the pak choi in a pan, and put to one side.

5 Cut the apple into small, fine matchsticks, and leave in the fridge.

6 Remove the squid from the freezer (if using this tenderising method) and cut into long, thin strips.

7 Sauté the squid strips in a pan of hot oil until they curl, then set aside.

8 Score the pig's ear on both sides and cut into small pieces.

9 Arrange the pieces of pig's ear in a row on the plate, alternating with the pak choi, and top it with the squid, then spoon over the sauce.

10 Scatter over the mustard sprouts and the apple matchsticks, dust the plate with curry powder, and then top with marigold flowers.

Tip

There are various ways to tenderise squid: freezing it before use softens it, as does pounding with a rolling pin. You can also try soaking it in milk for an hour.

MIGAS EXTREMEÑAS
'Crumbs' from Extremadura

The stunning town of Cáceres, in one of the most remote corners of Spain, sits in farming country, and its dishes reflect that. Migas were created by shepherds to keep them nourished all day.

Like so many Spanish dishes, *migas* has its roots in the long days of walking that shepherds would endure to find fresh pastureland for their sheep, carrying the bare bones of a meal in their pockets to be cooked over an open fire. These basic ingredients largely consisted of leftover bread (*migas* means breadcrumbs), salt and garlic, which would be added to whatever vegetables could be found along the way, and later came to include cured ham and sausages. There are regional variations from Aragon, from Andalucía, but the Extremadura version is generally considered to be the classic one. 'We have other well-known dishes in the region,' says Alejandro Jarrones Arias, 'But *migas* and Extremadura are inextricably connected.'

El Figón de Eustaquio has been honouring this connection for over half a century. Opened by Eustaquio Blanco in 1947, and still run by the same family, it has fed a staggering amount of visitors to the picturesque medieval town of Cáceres. In that time, the menu has changed little. 'That's what we're about' confirms Alejandro. 'I would say about 80% of the dishes have stayed the same, but that's why people come here.'

'The important thing with *migas* is to keep it moving in the pan so all the crumbs are soaked in the juice,' Alejandro explains, 'and the shepherds had plenty of time for this. There's a saying: *"Las migas del pastor, cuanto más vueltas mejor; las del gañán, a las dos vueltas están."'* With the shepherd's crumbs, the more they are stirred the better; with the farmhand's crumbs, a couple of times will do.

Chef // Alejandro Jarrones Arias
Location // El Figón de Eustaquio, Cáceres

MIGAS EXTREMEÑAS
'Crumbs' from Extremadura

Serves 4

Preparation & cooking time 30min

2 tbsp olive oil
4 cloves of garlic, sliced finely
1 red pepper, diced finely
150g (5¼oz) pancetta
150g (5¼oz) chorizo
1 tsp of pimentón dulce (sweet paprika)
250ml (8¾ fl oz) chicken or beef stock, or 250ml
    (8¾ fl oz) water with salt
500g (1lb) breadcrumbs
4 eggs (optional)

1 Heat the oil in a frying pan, and fry the garlic and pepper. When the garlic begins to brown, add the pancetta and the chorizo.

2 Once it has cooked, after 5–10 minutes, add the paprika and stir, then quickly add the stock to make sure the paprika doesn't burn.

3 Add the breadcrumbs and combine over a low heat, stirring constantly, until the bread has soaked up all the juice.

4 You can serve with a fried egg on top of each portion, if desired.

Tip

Native to Extremadura, pimentón de la Vera is a pungent smoky paprika, generally considered to be the best you can find. It's available in Spanish delicatessens and even large supermarkets.

COCIDO MADRILEÑO
Madrid meat & chickpea stew

Madrid's signature dish is the perfect antidote to its bracing winter days: a steaming chickpea stew brimming with flavour, slow-cooked over coals and served in two parts.

'This place is a museum!' exclaims Lola Soto Sánchez, gesturing around her at the tiled and wood-panelled dining room, the oil paintings, kitsch lanterns, wall friezes and framed photos, slightly askew. La Bola has been owned by the same family since 1870, when the *cocido* (stew) – Madrid's signature dish – was served in three sittings: the first was at noon, for the workers, and cost 1.15 pesetas; the second, at 1pm, contained chicken, cost 1.25 pesetas and was aimed at students; and the last, at 2pm, was for the unlikely combination of 'journalists and senators', and had red meat in it. The price of this final feast is not known.

The menu these days is more varied, but most visitors still come for the hearty *cocido*. Lola, who has worked here for 'I don't want to tell you how long,' estimates that they serve 35,000 of them every year. The production is militarily organised, wonderfully simple, and has barely changed over the decades – Lola pours the chickpeas, ham, pork, chicken and potato into a terracotta jug, covers all the ingredients in water, and then arranges the jugs in rows over a grill fuelled with oak wood, where they are occasionally topped up with stock made from the same ingredients.

'We encourage customers to come and see what's happening behind the scenes. Ours must be the most visited kitchen in Madrid,' laughs Mara Verdasco, whose family has run the restaurant since its inception.

A prototype for slow food, the *cocido* simmers away for four or five hours, and is served in three steaming parts – the stock is poured over noodles to make a soup, then the meat and chickpeas are served, along with a plate of garlicky cabbage and a side plate of tomato and cumin, along with pickles and spring onions. 'It's the best in the world,' beams Lola. 'Everybody says so.'

Chef //
Dolores (Lola) Soto Sánchez
Location //
La Bola, Madrid

COCIDO MADRILEÑO
Madrid meat & chickpea stew

Serves 4

Preparation & cooking time (not including soaking chickpeas) 4hr

800g (1¾lb) chickpeas, pre-soaked in water overnight, then rinsed and drained
4 ham bones
480g (1lb) beef shank
160g (5½oz) fatty pork belly
160g (5½oz) chorizo, chopped in large chunks
400g (14oz) chicken, quartered
approx 3L (5pt) water
160g (5½oz) potatoes, peeled & cut in half (quartered, if very large)
400g (14oz) cabbage, chopped
3–4 tbsp olive oil
3 cloves of garlic, sliced thinly
salt & pepper, to taste
200g (7oz) fideos or other short, fine noodles

1 Place the chickpeas, ham bones, beef shank, pork belly, chorizo and chicken in a large earthenware dish and cover with water. Cook over a low heat for 4 hours, adding more water as required.

2 After 3 hours, add the potatoes to the stew.

3 In a separate pan, fry the garlic in the olive oil, then add the cabbage. Season to taste.

4 Drain the broth from the stock in step 1 and use to cook the noodles.

5 Serve the *cocido* in two stages: first the broth with the noodles, followed by the meat and chickpeas, accompanied by a side dish of the garlicky cabbage.

Tip

Serve the cocido with a side dish of grated tomatoes mixed with cumin seeds, guindilla (chilli) peppers, and spring onions.

LECHAZO
Roast milk-fed lamb

Sheep have been a mainstay of the central plains since time immemorial, both for wool and the tender meat of their suckling lambs, here roasted in a vast wood oven.

Part restaurant, part museum, the spectacular Parrilla de San Lorenzo is set in a 16th-century monastery building, with vaulted bare-brick dining rooms that drip with medieval art. Towering oil paintings sit beneath beams adorned with friezes, and there are carvings, polychrome altarpieces and ancient wooden sculptures at every turn. Centuries-old tiling runs along the walls and vast swathes of red velvet are draped over the windows. The real reason to come here, however, is the lamb.

Fernando Lorenzo's family have run the restaurant since it opened in 1988. 'I was born in a tiny town on the Meseta Castellana (Castilian Plateau),' he says, 'where one of the things we most looked forward to was roast lamb. The geography of this part of Castilla is perfect for breeding sheep.'

In La Parrilla they use Churra sheep, the oldest known breed in Spain, and valued for the quality of their wool as well as their meat. 'There are many ways you cook *lechazo*,' says Fernando, 'But the very best is in a wood-fired oven, and oak wood gives the best flavour. It manages to be tasty and light at the same time, because we keep it simple – no other ingredients apart from water and salt.'

'When I was a boy and we wanted to make this dish, we'd just go and ask a local shepherd – there weren't many butchers' shops around in those days. The shepherd would choose a lamb from his flock and bring it to our house. Not all of us had ovens, though, so a lot of people would take meat to the local bakery and the bakers would put it in their wood ovens there. To this day I can still remember the smell as it came freshly roasted out of the oven.'

Chef //
Juan Bañez Valerio
Location //
La Parrilla de San
Lorenzo, Valladolid

LECHAZO
Roast milk-fed lamb

Serves 4

Preparation & cooking time 2hr

½ milk-fed lamb (ideally Churra lamb)
salt
1L (2pt) water

1 Pre-heat the oven to 200°C (390°F).

2 Put the lamb in a terracotta dish with the ribs facing upwards. Sprinkle with some salt and water to help make the skin crispy.

3 Roast for 1 hour and 30 minutes, then turn the lamb and cook for another 30 minutes until the skin is golden.

YEMAS DE SANTA TERESA
Candied egg yolks

Spain's convents have long been synonymous with confectionery, and at her Ávila bakery Isabel Hernández has recreated some deliciously indulgent recipes, particularly these distinctive yellow balls, which commemorate a saint.

Convents and monasteries have always played an important role in Spanish affairs, not least because of historical ties to the aristocracy, who would once pack off their unmarried or disgraced daughters to a convent, along with a handsome wedge of funding. Traditionally these convents would be called upon to provide cakes and sweetmeats for the feasts of the nobility, and this grew to become a cottage industry on an immense scale. To this day, closed orders of nuns all over Spain sell confectionery via revolving wooden turntables that allow them to remain invisible behind the convent walls.

Crumbly *polvorónes* (almond cookies), delicate wafers and flaky *palmiers* (palm-leaf-shaped crisp pastries) are all wrapped in waxed paper and swivelled through the turntables from sacred ground into the temporal world outside, along with the rich, sweet yellow balls known as *yemas* (egg yolks) *de Santa Teresa*. The origins of the name are disputed, but mostly believed to be a canny bit of medieval marketing, commemorating Spain's best-loved saint of the age. In Ávila, Saint Teresa's birthplace and where she founded the order of barefoot Carmelite nuns, *yemas* are ubiquitous.

'The basic recipe hasn't changed much,' says Isabel Hernández, in the patisserie set up by her grandfather. 'Egg yolk, sugar and a little lemon. But everyone adds their own touch – some bakers add cinnamon, others glaze them... Ours are handmade, so there are always slight variations.' She rolls them into balls, dusting them with icing sugar and placing them in small paper cases. These, in turn, are arranged in pretty boxes, stamped with the council of Castilla y León's hard-won seal of approval. 'There are certain things any visitor to Ávila shouldn't miss out on,' says Isabel. 'Wandering around the palaces and convents, but also picking up a box of these to take back home.'

Chef //
Isabel Hernández Vallejo
Location //
Bollería y Pastelería
Mariano Hernández, Ávila

YEMAS DE SANTA TERESA
Candied egg yolks

Serves 4

*Preparation & cooking time 30min,
not including chilling time*

10 egg yolks
125g (4½oz) granulated sugar
squeeze of lemon juice
icing sugar for decoration

1 Gently whisk the egg yolks in a bowl with the sugar. Add a squeeze of lemon juice.

2 Put the mixture into a saucepan and cook over a low heat, stirring continuously to prevent sticking, and ensuring that it doesn't boil. Remove from the heat when the mixture begins to pull away from the sides of the pan.

3 Once the mixture has cooled, turn it onto a board lightly dusted with icing sugar and roll into long strips. Cut each strip into small pieces, and roll each piece into a ball.

4 Put the rolled balls on a tray or a plate and allow to chill for 24 hours in the fridge.

Tip

Adding a squeeze of lemon juice to the whisked egg yolks and sugar helps to cut the sweetness.

CHURROS
Fried dough sticks dusted in sugar

Breakfasting on crunchy, piping hot churros dipped in hot chocolate is one of Spain's great pleasures, and madrileños have queued outside the Chocolatería San Ginés to do so since 1894.

The guilty little secret of the much vaunted Mediterranean diet, churros are as dear to the Spanish heart as tortilla, paella or patatas bravas. The nearest thing the country has to perennial street food, churros are served in paper cones from hole-in-the-wall kitchens and carried to cafes, where they are dunked in cups of dark, sweet chocolate the consistency of paste.

Churrerías that function as cafes are a rarity nowadays, the one celebrated exception being the much loved Chocolatería San Ginés, down a picturesque alleyway in the heart of old Madrid. Granted a unique exceptional permit from the City Hall, it opens 24 hours a day, 365 days a year, and its marble-topped tables and green leather banquettes have seen night owls of every type. In the late 19th and early 20th century these were writers, artists and other bohemian types (it is mentioned in several literary works of the period), and in the cosy vaulted downstairs salon the *tertulias* (artistic gatherings) would go on until dawn. It still attracts its fair share of celebrity visitors, and in the black-and-white photos dotted around the walls you'll see Richard Gere, Paloma Picasso, Javier Bardem, Pedro Almodóvar and countless others.

Since La Movida (The Movement) when post-Franco Madrid famously let its hair down with an outpouring of creativity and high jinks, the San Ginés has become inextricably linked to emblematic Madrid nightclub Joy Eslava nearby, and still now there is something of a rush hour for churros and chocolate at sunrise, as exhausted party animals seek to refuel before the journey home.

Despite the industrial quantities demanded by Chocolatería San Ginés' regular clientele, the churros batter is still mixed by hand, to get a better sense of when it's ready. 'There's nothing very complicated about making them, though' says master *churrero*, Dani Real. 'It's just flour and water.' Judging by the queue snaking out of the door, there may be more to it than that.

Chef //
Daniel Real
Location //
Chocolatería San
Ginés, Madrid

CHURROS
Fried dough sticks dusted in sugar

Serves 4

Preparation & cooking time 30min

250ml (8¾ fl oz) water
a pinch of salt
225g (8oz) plain flour, sifted
approx 1L (34 fl oz) olive oil for frying
sprinkle of sugar, to serve

1 Heat the water in a large saucepan with a pinch of salt.

2 Once the water begins to boil, reduce the heat, and add the flour slowly, whisking continuously, until it forms a ball. Leave aside until cool.

3 In a heavy pan with high sides, heat enough oil to cover the churros over a medium-high heat. When the oil reaches 180°C (350°F), pipe in the churro batter in short lengths, or long spirals that can be cut when cooking.

4 Fry until golden, and then drain on paper towels to remove any excess oil.

5 Sprinkle with sugar and serve with hot chocolate.

Tip

If you don't have a churrera (a tube with a nozzle for making churros), you can use a piping bag with a wide nozzle.

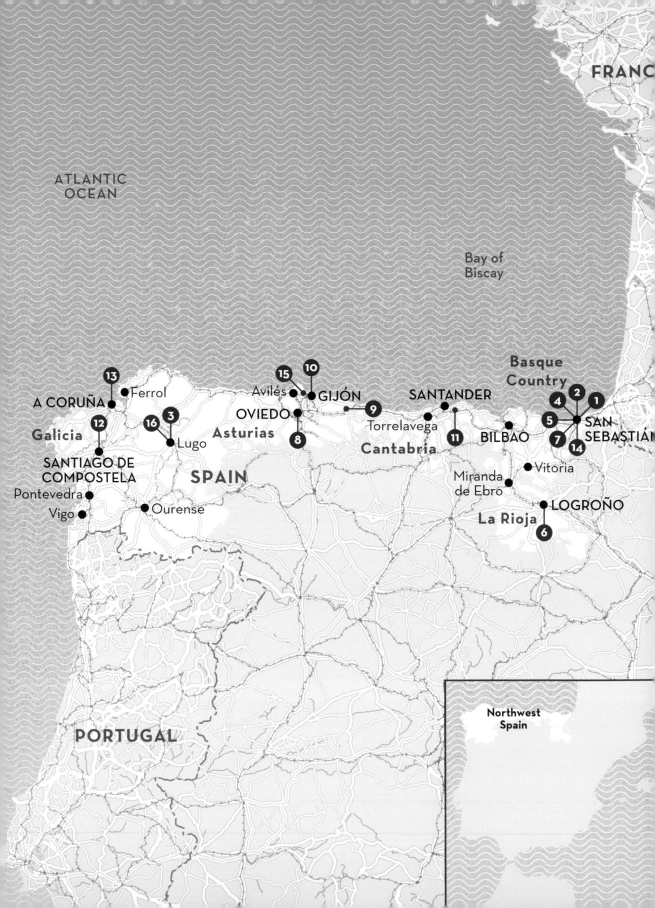

NORTHWEST SPAIN

Galicia, with its breathtaking variety of seafood, and Asturias, Spain's dairy producers par excellence, flank the birthplace of Spanish haute cuisine – the Basque Country. Still a hotbed of culinary talent, its bright young stars work alongside the doyens of gastronomy to perfect the recipes of old and adapt them for the 21st century.

TRES PINTXOS
Three Basque tapas
page 150

PULPO CON HOJAS DE BERZA SALTEADAS Y TOCINETA
Octopus with savoy cabbage & streaky bacon
page 156

CALDO GALLEGO
Ham, bean & turnip-top broth
page 160

MERLUZA AL VAPOR CON PLANKTON
Steamed hake with plankton
page 164

TXANGURRO A LA DONOSTIARRA
Stuffed crab in the style of San Sebastián
page 168

PATATAS A LA RIOJANA
Rioja-style potatoes
page 172

PURRUSALDA
Leek & potato broth
page 176

FABADA ASTURIANA
Asturian bean stew
page 180

REVUELTO DE CEBOLLA Y CABRALES SOBRE TORTA CRUJIENTE DE MAÍZ
Crispy corn bread with onion & Cabrales
page 184

PIXÍN CON TXANGURRO Y ALIOLI LIGERO
Monkfish with spider crab & light alioli
page 188

CARICO MONTAÑÉS
Bean stew
page 192

PULPO A LA MUGARDESA
Octopus in a Mugardos style
page 196

VIEIRAS A LA GALLEGA
Galician-style scallops
page 200

PANTXINETA
Almond cream pastry
page 204

CREMA DE ARROZ CON LECHE REQUEMADA
Scorched rice pudding
page 208

TARTA DE SANTIAGO
St James' cake
page 212

TRES PINTXOS
Three Basque tapas

Of the new breed of tapas chefs, Edorta Lamo gives old favourites a funky touch in his relaxed bar, A Fuego Negro, where music shares top billing with sublime cooking.

From the Basque word for 'skewer', a *pintxo* is generally a tapa speared with a cocktail stick and served on top of a slice of baguette. The purpose of the cocktail stick is twofold – it holds the elements together and, in an eminently civilised system, shows the bartender how many you've eaten when you bring your plate up to pay.

'The Gilda [see recipe] is the oldest and – in my opinion – the best of San Sebastián's gastronomic creations,' says Edorta Lamo, chef at A Fuego Negro, reviewing his favourite *pintxos*. 'It's very simple, but it's the perfect mouthful, reminiscent of the tinned *conservas* they used to serve in bars, and creating the perfect equilibrium between the acidity of the *guindillas* (pickled chillies) and the oily sweetness of the anchovies and olives. In our version we wanted to create an aperitif as a 'shot' with Basque *txakoli* wine.'

'When the bars started offering something more than the *conservas* or the Gildas, they started to make the little creations that still adorn the bars today, like the "egg, prawn and mayonnaise" pintxo, which was half a boiled egg on a little slice of fried bread, with mayonnaise and a prawn, speared with a toothpick, on top. With ours, we wanted to pay homage to these but with a gastronomic edge. We use a quail's egg, soft-boiled, a really good prawn, scalded, and an edible toothpick, and a light, foamy mayonnaise. To intensify the taste of the prawn we make a reduction with the heads.'

'Squid are normally served in battered rings, but too many bars these days serve frozen ones of dubious origin. We make them using a traditional stew of squid in ink, then we blend it and use it to fill circular moulds to mimic the original shape. Once they're frozen we dip them in batter and fry them.'

Chef //
Edorta Lamo
Location //
A Fuego Negro,
San Sebastián

BLACK RABAS
Black squid rings

Serves 6

Preparation & cooking time 1½hr

1kg (2¼lb) squid in ink
2 cloves of garlic, chopped finely
1 onion, chopped finely
1 green pepper, chopped finely
1 leek, chopped finely
olive oil for frying
2 ripe tomatoes, peeled & chopped
50ml (1¾ fl oz) white wine
300ml (10½ fl oz) fish stock
pinch of salt, to taste
1L (1¾pt) tepid water
50g (1¾oz) fresh yeast
750g (1¾lb) flour, plus extra for
*   squid dipping*
50ml (1¾ fl oz) olive oil, for deep frying

1 Clean and chop the squid, keeping the ink to one side.

2 Sauté the garlic, onion, pepper and leek in a large saucepan with a splash of olive oil. When cooked, add the chopped tomatoes, and then the squid.

3 Add the wine, immediately followed by the fish stock.

4 When it comes to the boil, add the ink and cook over a medium heat for 20–30 minutes.

5 Add salt to taste, then blend with a liquidiser/hand blender, strain into a bowl, and leave to cool.

6 Pour the cooled squid mixture into a piping bag, and fill silicone moulds. Chill the moulds in the freezer.

7 Make the tempura by adding a splash of the tepid water to the yeast in a large bowl, and then very slowly add the rest of the water and the flour. Leave in a warm place for 30 minutes for the mixture to ferment.

8 Remove the frozen squid rings from the moulds.

9 Dust the frozen rings in flour, dip them in tempura and deep fry in olive oil.

'REVIVAL' DE GAMBAS Y HUEVOS
Prawn & egg mayonnaise 'revival'

12 fresh Huelva prawns (or any medium-
   sized prawns)
1½L (2½pt) culinary sea water
   (or salted water)
1 tbsp barbecue sauce
1 frozen baguette
2-3 tbsp olive oil for frying
12 quail eggs
3 egg yolks
80ml (2¾ fl oz) milk
340ml (12 fl oz) sunflower oil
80ml (2¾ fl oz) olive oil
2 tsp lemon juice
1 rounded tsp salt
50ml (1¾ fl oz) cream
cocktail sticks, to serve
parsley, to garnish

1 Scald the prawns in the boiling sea water, and then plunge into iced water. Remove the prawn heads and reserve. Discard the rest of the shell except for the tip of the tail.

2 Put the prawn heads in a saucepan over a high heat. Add the barbecue sauce and cover with iced water. Crush the heads with a wooden spoon and let the mixture simmer for two hours.

3 Remove the prawn-heads mixture from the heat, cover with cling film/plastic wrapping and leave to infuse until cool. Strain the mixture into a bowl and set aside.

4 Cut very thin slices of half the frozen baguette, soak them with the prawn-heads mixture and place on a baking sheet in an oven on a low heat (50°C/120°F) until they dry out. Blend the baked baguette slices into breadcrumbs and set aside.

5 Cut the other half of the baguette into slices about 1cm (½in) thick. Trim off the crusts, and fry in the olive oil. Set aside.

6 Boil the quail eggs for 2 minutes in salted water, stirring occasionally with a slotted spoon. Cool them in iced water, peel the shells, and leave the eggs to sit in salted water (10g/⅓oz salt per L/1¾pt of water).

7 For the mayonnaise, beat the egg yolks with the milk and add the sunflower and olive oils very slowly, beating until an emulsion is informed. Then add the lemon juice, the salt and cream.

8 Coat the 12 fresh prawns in the breadcrumbs soaked in prawn-heads mixture.

9 Carefully insert a cocktail stick into the middle of each piece of fried bread. Spear a quail egg and a prawn on to each stick. Serve in a bowl with the mayonnaise and decorate with a sprig of parsley.

GILDA

18 small pickled *piparras* or *guindillas*
    (pickled chillies)
6 large green pitted olives
6 salted anchovies
250ml (8½ fl oz) txakoli or dry, sparkling
    white wine

1 Insert *piparras* into the pitted olives, wrap around anchovies and spear with a cocktail stick (see Tip).

2 Fill a small, chilled shot glass with wine and balance the speared olive on top.

> ## *Tip*
>
> *At A Fuego Negro, edible cocktail sticks are made in custom-made moulds, but a less perfect effect can be achieved by mixing 300g (10½ oz) mannitol and 30g (1oz) icing sugar together and cooking in a saucepan on a low heat until the mixture turns golden. Spread out on a baking tray to cool and then cut with a sharp knife.*

PULPO CON HOJAS DE BERZA SALTEADAS Y TOCINETA

Octopus with savoy cabbage & streaky bacon

San Sebastián's new breed of inventive tapas bars are changing the scene for those who enjoy impulsive dining. This sticky, garlicky tapa of octopus and cabbage proves its mettle.

The undisputed gastronomic capital of Spain, San Sebastián has more Michelin stars per capita than Paris, London or New York, but you don't need especially deep pockets to eat like a king here – the city's *pintxo* (tapas) bars put fine-dining within the reach of everybody. The Parte Vieja (Old Town) bristles with them, particularly along the Calle 31 de Agosto, where you can graze all night on tiny morsels of heaven that will only cost a couple of euros. Many of these bars have been around for decades, their burnished counters groaning with plates of piled up *pintxos*, to which you just help yourself.

In recent years, however, there has appeared a new breed of *pintxo* bar, every bit as affordable and convivial, but with a slightly more avant-garde approach to tapas, and one where these are made to order. One such is La Cuchara de San Telmo, set up by Alex Montiel, a Catalan who refuses to limit himself to the cuisine of any one Spanish region, and sees exactly that attitude as one of the strengths of Basque gastronomy; an openness to new ideas and flavours.

This dish, one of La Cuchara's most popular, combines various influences. 'Octopus is often seen as a Galician thing,' he says, 'But in San Sebastián there is a huge Galician community, they have an entire neighbourhood, Trintxerpe, which is known as the "fifth Galician province".' He waxes lyrical about cabbage, describing it as 'the humble princess of winter vegetables' in the north of Spain, and is a keen adopter of the *refrito* (oil in which garlic has previously been fried). The final dish is the perfect medley of flavour and texture, the cabbage dotted with chewy little nuggets of garlic, the seared tentacles both tender and melt-in-the-mouth.

Chef //
Paula Ale
Location //
La Cuchara de San Telmo,
San Sebastián

PULPO CON HOJAS DE BERZA SALTEADAS Y TOCINETA

Octopus with savoy cabbage & streaky bacon

Serves 4

Preparation & cooking time 2hr, not including octopus cooling time

4L (7pt) water
3 bay leaves
8 cloves of garlic
1 tbsp Sichuan pepper
handful of sea salt
1 octopus
8 savoy cabbage leaves
1 handful parsley leaves, chopped finely
1 sprig of thyme
1 tbsp dried oregano
½ tsp ground Espelette pepper
  (or chilli pepper)
1½ tbsp apple cider vinegar
150ml (5¼ fl oz) sunflower oil
8 slices of streaky bacon, preferably
  uncured
approx 150ml (5¼ fl oz) olive oil, for
  frying garlic & octopus

Tip

It's a good idea to leave the octopus to cool for as long as possible, or even to make it the day before.

1 Put the water to heat in a saucepan, and add the bay leaves, one of the garlic cloves (chopped), Sichuan pepper, and a handful of salt.

2 Clean the octopus thoroughly under running water, cleaning out all the dirt from the tentacles and the inside of the head.

3 When the water starts boiling, dip the octopus slowly in the water until the end of the legs contract, then remove. Do this three times, and then submerge it completely in the water.

4 Simmer for about 45 minutes. Pinch the upper part of the tentacles and below the head to check if tender. Remove the octopus and put it on a tray to cool.

5 Wash the cabbage and cut each leaf in two. Place in boiling water (enough to cover the cabbage) with a pinch of salt. Remove when the leaves are tender, but still green, and plunge into iced water to ensure they don't cook any more. Set aside.

6 Finely chop three of the cloves of garlic and mix with the chopped parsley. Add the leaves from the sprig of thyme, the oregano and the Espelette pepper. Mix with the apple cider vinegar and the sunflower oil, and allow the mixture to sit for 20 minutes to intensify the flavours.

7 Fry the bacon in a pan until it sweats and turns transparent, then set aside (keep it warm).

8 Heat 2 tbsp olive oil in a frying pan, slice the remaining cloves of garlic, and fry until golden, then remove the garlic and set aside. Reserve the oil for serving.

9 Take four octopus legs and cut pieces of about 12cm (4½in) each for each plate. Fry the octopus in olive oil. The rest of the octopus can be frozen and used at a later date.

10 Add some of the toasted garlic slices to the cabbage.

11 To serve, arrange a cabbage leaf on the bottom of the plate, then top with a slice of bacon, then another cabbage leaf and another slice of bacon. Crown with the octopus, sprinkle over some salt, then decorate with the rest of the toasted garlic slices and a few drops of the oil in which they were fried.

CALDO GALLEGO
Ham, bean & turnip-top broth

In the cool, damp climate that sets Galicia apart from the rest of the country, this steaming broth makes for a gutsy pick-me-up, and is relatively easy to replicate at home.

Within Spain, the region of Galicia is best known for its superb seafood, which is exported to every corner of the country. Outside Spain, however, its most famous dish is the *caldo gallego*, along with its close relation, *lacón con grelos*. Both use two peculiarly Galician ingredients – *lacón* (cured pork shoulder) and *grelos*, which are turnip tops, specifically those that have gone *grelado* (to seed).

Turnips, in Galicia, are viewed as food for livestock, while their leaves are used in all manner of dishes. 'They are seasonal, however,' says chef Rubén Cirés Molina. 'So kale or cabbage is a perfectly acceptable alternative. But if you do use turnip tops, you need to briefly blanch them in boiling water to draw out any bitterness.'

Another curious ingredient of the *caldo gallego* is *unto*, a type of cured lard. The climate of the region doesn't really lend itself to dry curing, so this is often done over the embers of a fire, which gives the *unto* a smoky quality (although, again, normal lard is also fine). 'People would cure it in their fireplaces at home,' says Nicolás Vázquez, the owner of Restaurante Campos in Lugo. 'This was a dish that started in the little *pueblos* of Galicia, and all the raw materials were produced locally, from the vegetables to the pork.'

'When my grandparents set up the restaurant in 1952,' he goes on, 'It was just a typical *taberna*, and people would bring their own food that would be cooked here. Eventually my grandparents started making and selling it themselves and, although we've updated things a bit, we still use some of the old recipes. These days we reproduce dishes from all over the Mediterranean, but our prime ingredients are always *gallego*. We've been with some of our producers for over 30 years.'

Chef //
Rubén Cirés Molina
Location //
Restaurante Campos, Lugo

CALDO GALLEGO
Ham, bean & turnip-top broth

Serves 6

Preparation & cooking time 1hr, 30min

200g (7oz) haricot beans
500g (1lb) pancetta, cut into two pieces
250g (8¾oz) lacón (or pork shoulder)
1 beef bone
6L (10½pt) mineral water
500g (1lb) unto (Galician lard) or regular lard
  if unavailable
3 large potatoes, peeled & roughly chopped
  into small chunks
3 handfuls of turnip tops (or kale or cabbage
  if unavailable)
salt, to taste

1 Put the beans, pancetta, *lacón* (or pork shoulder) and the beef bone in a large saucepan, and cover with the cold mineral water. Bring to the boil and cook for 1 hour and 30 minutes.

2 Add the *unto* (or lard), along with the potatoes. If using turnip tops, blanch them briefly in boiling water and add to the beans and meat. Kale or cabbage can be added directly.

3 Cook for another 10 minutes and then remove the *lacón* (or pork shoulder), the *unto* (or skim off the lard) and the beef bone. Season to taste, and serve.

Tip

Once the water has come to the boil, tip in a glass of cold water two or three times during the cooking process. This trick is known as asustando las alubias (scaring the beans), and means that the outer skin won't become too soft and fall apart but the insides will cook thoroughly.

MERLUZA AL VAPOR CON PLANKTON
Steamed hake with plankton

On a wind-lashed hilltop outside San Sebastián, Pedro Subijana shows just why he is considered a founding father of modern Spanish cooking, with a dish as surprising as it is delicious.

It is no exaggeration to say that Spanish gastronomy would not have reached the dizzying heights it occupies today without the efforts of Pedro Subijana. Along with Juan Mari Arzak at nearby Arzak, he spearheaded the 1970s revolution that ended in *nueva cocina*, a new type of cooking using groundbreaking techniques and ingredients that would not have been considered just a few years earlier.

Fast forward 40 years, and his cooking is still considered pioneering. His secret lies not only in a broad-minded outlook and willingness to consider the most outlandish of combinations but a solid grounding in the classic ways of doing things, and above all an abiding love for the native dishes of his Basque homeland.

This dish encapsulates that delicate balance. On the one hand it honours a timeless classic, the hake *al pil pil*. The curious name comes from the sound that the tiny bubbles of albumen make as they escape the fish as it cooks – here those bubbles are rendered as minuscule balls of egg white, with the briefest hint of the garlic and parsley used in the age-old recipe. For most chefs this would be enough, but Pedro's fascination with the latest developments means that he then teams this other-worldly confection with a pesto made of plankton, inspired by the recent advances made with this abundant and unexploited foodstuff by his friend and celebrated chef Ángel León in Málaga.

In combination with the succulent oyster leaf, these elements create a harmonious experience that combines textures and flavours and, for the diner, evokes the presence of the sea, the same stormy sea that crashes dramatically on the rocks just below the floor-to-ceiling windows of Akelarre's dining room and dictates so much of what happens in his serenely calm kitchen.

Chef //
Pedro Subijana
Location //
Akelarre, San Sebastián

MERLUZA AL VAPOR
CON PLANKTON
Steamed hake with plankton

Serves 4

Preparation & cooking time 30min

For the plankton pesto
½ tsp garlic, peeled & chopped
100g (3½oz) Parmesan, grated
200g (7oz) toasted pine nuts
5g (¼oz) garum (or anchovy extract)
½ tsp plankton dissolved in 200ml (7 fl oz) olive oil
½ tsp plankton dissolved in 200ml (7 fl oz) water
4 oyster leaves, to serve

For the caviar
whites of 3 eggs
½ tsp grated garlic
½ tsp finely chopped parsley
olive oil, for frying

For the hake
100g (3½oz) salt
1L (1¾pt) water
4 x 150g (5¼oz) skinless hake steaks (or any
   meaty white sea fish, such as cod/haddock)
4 sheets marbled kombu seaweed

1 Make the plankton pesto by putting the pesto ingredients (garlic, Parmesan, toasted pine nuts, garum, and the plankton that's dissolved in olive oil), into a liquidiser and blend well. Mix in the plankton-water solution into the pesto until it forms an emulsion. Strain the pesto into a bowl and reserve.

2 To make the 'caviar', blend the egg whites in a liquidiser. Mix in the grated garlic and leave to infuse for an hour, and then add the finely chopped parsley. Heat the olive oil in a frying pan over a low heat. Add drops of the caviar mix using a pipette and cook for one minute before removing and placing in a bowl with clean oil. Repeat until all the egg whites have been cooked. Set side.

3 Prepare the hake fillets by dissolving the salt in the water, and placing the hake in the salted water for 5 minutes. Remove, drain and pat dry lightly with kitchen paper. Lay a piece of seaweed over the hake skin.

4 Steam the hake for 2½ minutes, and then place each fillet on top of a spoonful of the caviar.

5 Put a dot of plankton pesto on the plate, and draw a comb through it to make a rippled effect. Place an oyster leaf on top, and serve.

TXANGURRO A LA DONOSTIARRA

Stuffed crab in the style of San Sebastián

An intensely rich and flavourful dish, crab cooked 'San Sebastián style' betrays its French roots, but at the same time is an embodiment of Basque cuisine.

'**S**an Sebastián is known for many different dishes, but only one is allowed to bear the surname *donostiarra* [meaning of/from San Sebastián],' says Juan Carlos Caro. This much-feted dish was invented over a century ago by chef and food writer Felix Ibarguren, who was highly influenced by French chefs and Escoffier in particular, and created this dish as a local version of lobster *a l'américaine*. It is often described as the only Basque dish that owes its origins to haute cuisine.

The secret, according to Juan Carlos, is in a really good *sauce américaine*, the velvety bisque that he says 'should be rich, of a deep hue, and intensify the taste of the sea when you mix it with the crab.' The origin of its name is disputed; some say it used to be served to American passengers on ocean liners, others are inclined to believe it originated in the US, while many food writers insist the correct term is *armoricaine*, from Armorica, the ancient name for Brittany.

The dish itself is dear to most *donostiarras*, and Juan Carlos himself remembers eating it with his parents in the iconic (now closed) restaurant Casa Nicolasa as a child. There it was occasionally served with spider crab (*txangurra*, with an 'a'), but Juan Carlos' preference is for brown, or edible, crab, prepared with the utmost care. He vaccum-packs the live crab before lowering into a warm bath, around 70°C (160°F), for 40 minutes. This, he says, is the most humane way, for the crab will slip gently into unconsciousness, while the vacuum-packing ensures it will lose none of its juices in the cooking process.

Unusually for a Spanish chef, and perhaps because of his experience in French kitchens, Juan Carlos tends to favour butter over olive oil, and it is this that gives the dish its intensely creamy flavour. 'It's been around for a very long time,' he says, 'but to my mind, this is a dish that will always feel modern.'

Chef //
Juan Carlos Caro
Location //
Zelai Txiki, San Sebastián

TXANGURRO A LA DONOSTIARRA

Stuffed crab in the style of San Sebastián

Serves 4

Preparation time & cooking 1hr, but coral wafers prepared two days in advance

For the crab

2 brown crabs
20g (¾oz) of salt per litre of water used (will vary)
2 spring onions
1 carrot
100ml (3½ fl oz) olive oil
1 knob of butter
50ml (2 fl oz) brandy (preferably Armagnac)

For the sauce américaine

1 carrot, chopped
2 onions, chopped
1 leek
3 tbsp olive oil, for frying
2 tomatoes, quartered
300g (10½oz) heads of crawfish, prawns or similar shellfish
50ml (2 fl oz) brandy (preferably Armagnac)
300ml (10½ fl oz) fish stock or fumet
30g (1oz) rice

For the wafers

100g (3½oz) white rice
1 tbsp olive oil
crab coral from the 2 brown crabs
300ml (10½ fl oz) water
200ml (7oz) sunflower oil for deep frying

1 Heat enough water to immerse the crabs, adding 20g (¾oz) of salt per litre of water. When the water begins to boil, add the crabs and cook for 12 minutes. Remove the crabs and plunge into iced water for 8 minutes to stop them from cooking further.

2 Chop the spring onions and carrot, and sauté in a pan with olive oil and butter.

3 Peel the crabs, removing the coral to use in the wafers.

4 Add the crab meat to the sautéed vegetables, flambé the brandy in a ladle by carefully setting fire to it with a match or a lighter, add to the crab mixture, and set aside.

5 For the *sauce américaine*, roughly chop the carrot, onion and leek, and sauté in olive oil. Add the quartered tomatoes, the tinned tomatoes and the shellfish shells.

6 Flambé the mixture with brandy (as per step 4), and add the fish stock and then the rice. Bring to the boil and continue to cook until the rice is tender. Blend the mixture to make a creamy sauce, and season to taste.

7 Mix the sauce with the crab meat and vegetables, then stuff the crab shells.

8 To make the wafers, stir the white rice grains in the olive oil, then add the coral and water, and cook until the rice is well done. Put in a blender, and then strain into a bowl. The cream produced should be spread very thinly on baking paper and left to dry in a warm dry place for two days. Break into uneven pieces, and fry in sunflower oil. The wafers are ready when they float to the top of the oil.

9 Put the stuffed crab into a pre-heated oven at 200°C (390°F) to brown. Decorate with pieces of the wafer, and serve.

Tip

Professional chefs cook the spider crabs slowly by putting them in vacuum-sealed bags and cooking sous-vide for 40 minutes in a bain-marie (or a Roner) at 70°C (160°F).

PATATAS A LA RIOJANA
Rioja-style potatoes

With its origins as a humble peasant dish, patatas a la riojana shot to fame after grand-père of modern French cuisine Paul Bocuse pronounced it exquisite.

Francis Paniego has been described as doing for the cuisine of La Rioja what Ferran Adrià did for Catalunya, or, long before that, what Juan-Mari Arzak did for the Basque Country. From the fifth generation of a culinary dynasty, he took over the reins of the family restaurant, Echaurren, eventually earning it two Michelin stars, and now oversees the kitchen at the fantastical Frank Gehry-designed winery for Marqués de Riscal. His latest venture is a slightly more modest tapas restaurant in Logroño, Tondeluna, where he brings old recipes to life.

'*Patatas a la riojana* has become a real classic in Riojan cuisine, but it hasn't actually been around that long. People round here won't like me saying this, but it's really a version of the *marmitako*, from the Basque coast, which uses potatoes and bonito – here we use chorizo, it's our equivalent of bonito, but from the land. The result is a dish that's really succulent, and full of flavour. It allows a lot of variation – some people make it with spicy chorizo, and others with red pepper, but my mother taught me to make it this way and this is how I like it.'

'It's a dish for the people, and easy to make, but it was actually Paul Bocuse who made it popular, at the end of the '70s. He came down to an event for the Cune winemakers, and they were showing him around and looking after him. But what do you cook for Paul Bocuse? There's no point trying to impress him, so the woman who cooked at the winery just made him a simple stew. He ate three plates in a row and said [questioning the need for his skills to be flown into the country], "Why did you bring me here when you already have something this exquisite?" After that it became our iconic dish.'

Chef //
Francis Paniego
Location //
Tondeluna, Logroño

PATATAS A LA RIOJANA
Rioja-style potatoes

Serves 6

Preparation & cooking time 40min

200g (7oz) lamb ribs, chopped into cubes
75ml (2½ fl oz) extra virgin olive oil
100g (3½oz) onion, peeled & chopped finely
2 cloves of garlic, peeled & chopped finely
1kg (2¼lb) potatoes, peeled & roughly chopped
1 bay leaf
1 tbsp pimentón dulce (sweet paprika)
1 tbsp crushed garlic mixed with finely chopped
   parsley
cold water
200g (7oz) chorizo, ideally from La Rioja,
   chopped into 1cm/½in chunks
1 pimiento choricero (dried red pepper – if none
   is available use roasted red pepper)
1 green pepper, roughly chopped
salt & pepper, to taste

1 In a large saucepan, fry the lamb in the olive oil until golden. When the lamb ribs are well toasted, add the chopped onion, and then, after two minutes, the garlic. Sauté everything together, taking care to ensure that the onions and garlic don't burn.

2 Add the potatoes, bay leaf, *pimentón dulce*, crushed garlic and parsley, and fry gently, ensuring that the potatoes don't stick.

3 Pour over enough cold water to cover the meat and vegetables, and bring to the boil. When it starts to boil, add the chorizo, the *pimiento choricero* and the chopped green pepper.

4 Bring to the boil again, then reduce the heat and cook slowly for about 20 minutes or until the potatoes are cooked through.

5 Season to taste and serve.

Tip

To chop the potatoes, first cut into large chunks, then break up by hand to give a rough surface texture. A similar effect is achieved by putting them in a pot with a lid and shaking so that they knock together. This releases the starch in a way that makes the stew thicker, though you can also simply add some flour to the simmering liquid.

PURRUSALDA
Leek & potato broth

If Basque cuisine specialises in one thing it's warming winter stews, and the purrusalda – a thick, steaming leek broth – is one of its best loved, as well as most versatile.

The *purrusalda* (or *porrusalda*, from the Euskera for 'leek' and 'broth') has been in the Basque canon for centuries, though there is a lot of disagreement about how it should be made and whether or not it should contain cod, and there is even more debate about its correct form. It can be served as a thick, robust stew, the vegetables left in chunks; it can be creamed, as in this recipe, or it can be served like a minestrone, a thin soup with diced vegetables. It's this very versatility that makes it so popular.

'It's a comforting dish, a winter dish,' says Patricio Fuentes, head chef at the San Sebastián Food cookery school. 'It has always been a dish of survival, too, something that could be rustled up with whatever vegetables were to hand in the *caseríos*.' *Caseríos* are the traditional half-timbered smallholdings that dot the Basque hillsides and still make up an essential element of local life. It is here that the best leeks are to be found, according to Patricio. 'Leeks should be fine, not thick. You only find those in the *caseríos* – those that are bred for mass production don't taste of anything.'

'The leeks are all-important, but aside from that the *purrusalda* can be whatever you want it to be. Add cod, or chicken, or keep it simple. Serve it as a soup or a main course, or spoon it alongside some fish.' A chronology of culinary history, the *purrusalda* reflects the changing tastes and availability of ingredients. Potatoes have not been around all that long in Spanish cooking, and carrots were only introduced into the dish at the end of the late century, when they became popular. 'When I teach this recipe I am giving a little lesson on Basque social and rural history,' Patricio adds.

Chef //
Patricio Fuentes
Location //
San Sebastián Food,
San Sebastián

PURRUSALDA
Leek & potato broth

Serves 4

Preparation & cooking time 45min

For the salted cod

200ml (7 fl oz) olive oil

2 cloves of garlic, whole

4 x 100g (3½oz) pieces of salted cod (pre-soaked, & with the skin left on)

For the purrusalda

100ml (3½ fl oz) olive oil

8 leeks, cleaned & chopped

2 medium potatoes, peeled & chopped

2 carrots, peeled & chopped

2 cloves of garlic, sliced

500ml (1pt) water

salt & pepper, to taste

fresh herbs/herb-infused olive oil, to serve

1 To first prepare the salted cod, warm 200ml of olive oil in a pan to 55°C (130°F) and fry the whole garlic cloves. Remove the garlic and cook the cod for 3 minutes on each side. Take the cod out, and put aside. Reserve the oil for later.

2 To prepare the *purrusalda*, heat 100ml of olive oil in a frying pan over a medium-high heat, adding the leeks, potatoes, carrots, sliced garlic cloves, and water. Cook until the vegetables are soft, then drain and reserve the stock.

3 Use a liquidiser to blend the vegetables, adding the stock slowly until you obtain a smooth cream. Season, and set aside.

4 Make a *pil-pil* sauce with the oil used to cook the cod in step 1. Pour most of the oil from the pan into a separate dish, using a straining spoon so that as much of the gelatin (visible as small bubbles) from the cod skin remains in the pan. Cook slowly over a low heat, stirring continuously with a sieve, until an emulsion is formed. Slowly add more of the reserved oil, and continue to stir vigorously until you have a thick sauce (about 15 or 20 minutes).

5 To serve, arrange the *purrusalda* in a deep dish with a piece of cod, then pour over the *pil-pil* sauce. Decorate with fresh herbs or herb-infused olive oil.

FABADA ASTURIANA
Asturian bean stew

The ultimate comfort food, fabada asturiana is a gutsy winter casserole, here given a deft touch by chef Luís Alberto Martínez at Oviedo's Casa Fermín.

After paella and gazpacho, the *fabada asturiana* – a rich, earthy bean stew – is Spain's most popular culinary export, and yet is fiercely local in more ways than one. 'It's a dish with a lot of personality,' says chef Luís Alberto Martínez, chef of the renowned Casa Fermín in Oviedo. 'And it's not always the same personality. It varies depending which zone of Asturias it's from, though it always evokes the region. That's why you should always uses *fabes asturianas* (Asturian white beans) if you can get hold of them.' The same holds true of the *compango*, the name given to the collection of different meats that is added to the stew. 'It should come from here, if you can find it, because ours is smoked.' This harks back to the days when the people of the region would cure meat by hanging it up in their fireplaces at home, the cool, damp Asturian climate making it difficult to use outhouses, as they would elsewhere in Spain.

'In fact, the *fabada* hasn't been around that long,' says Luís Alberto. 'The first time it was properly documented was in the 1930s, and even then it has changed a lot since. It's lighter now, and with less fat. We're no longer toiling in the fields, so we don't need the same kind of food. We need to be able to eat lunch and then go back to work, so it can't be too filling.'

One element that has made a difference is the recent popularity of fresh, rather than dried, *fabes*. 'They're healthier, easier to digest, more delicate and have a better flavour. You don't need to soak them, there's no tough skin and the beans don't break up when you cook them. The stew still has all the same characteristics, however. This dish is our calling card.'

Chef //
Luís Alberto Martínez
Location //
Casa Fermín, Oviedo

FABADA ASTURIANA
Asturian bean stew

Serves 4

Preparation & cooking time 2hr, not including soaking time for beans/lacón or resting time for stew

750g (1½lb) Asturian fabes beans (alternatively, use cannellini beans), presoaked for 24 hours in cold water
2 chorizos (approx 250g/½lb)
2 morcillas (blood sausages) (approx 250g/½lb)
500g (1lb) lacón (or pork shoulder); if using lacón, soak in cold water overnight to remove the salt
pinch of saffron
salt, to taste

1 Put the pre-soaked beans in a large saucepan with the chorizo and *morcilla* and cover with water. Bring to the boil, and skim off the froth at regular intervals.

2 Reduce the heat, and allow to simmer for about 90 minutes, adding water as required if necessary.

3 If using *lacón*, boil it in a separate saucepan for about 1 hour, then add to the beans. If you are using pork shoulder, cook it with the beans.

4 When the beans are cooked, add the saffron and remove from the heat. Leave to rest for at least an hour.

5 Cut the chorizo, *morcilla* and *lacón*/pork into chunks.

6 For this contemporary interpretation, serve the beans and the meat in separate dishes. For a traditional approach, serve them together. Season with salt, to taste.

Tip

If the stew is too liquid, take some of the beans out, puree them, and return to the pot to thicken the sauce. Bring to the boil briefly, and stir well.

REVUELTO DE CEBOLLA Y CABRALES SOBRE TORTA CRUJIENTE DE MAÍZ

Crispy corn bread with onion & Cabrales

These crispy corn puffs have been on the Asturian menu for centuries, with toppings that varied according to the times, the season and the means. Nacho Manzano shares one of his favourites.

The Asturian taste for corn began in the 17th century, as the explorers from Portugal and northwest Spain returned from the Americas bearing great sacks of it, and touting it as the solution to many of society's hardships. This campaign was so successful, and its consumption became so popular, that corn would later be banned in certain zones, for fear that the outbreak of scurvy was due to the abandonment of more nutritious foodstuffs.

'This is a dish that was born of necessity and poverty,' says Nacho Manzano, chef at Casa Marcial. 'After all, a *torto* is basically just flour. Originally it wouldn't even be fried, because oil was expensive, it was just cooked over the embers. But for people working in the fields all day it was a godsend – flour is filling. Not only that, but Asturias was already full of watermills, because we get a lot of rain, so it was easy to grind the corn down.'

Nacho learned to make them at an early age, watching his mother and grandmother in the kitchen of what was then the family home and later to become his restaurant. He and his sisters were born there. 'There are no hospitals for miles now,' he laughs. 'You can imagine what it was like then.' The family made ends meet by cooking to order, until they opened as a restaurant in 1993. A couple of decades later, Nacho has two Michelin stars under his belt, but his mother is still to be seen milling around the kitchen.

'My mother makes the best *tortos*,' says Nacho, somewhat enviously. 'She puts a lot of water in the dough, which makes it hard to work with but makes them puff up more and brings out the taste of the corn, I've no idea why. It makes it sweeter. They're spectacular.'

Chef //
Nacho Manzano
Location //
Casa Marcial, Parres

REVUELTO DE CEBOLLA Y CABRALES SOBRE TORTA CRUJIENTE DE MAÍZ

Crispy corn bread with onion & Cabrales

Serves 4

Preparation & cooking time 2hr 30 min, not including 6hr for dough to rest

For the tortos
¾ tsp salt
200g (7oz) cornflour
60g (2oz) flour
20ml (¾ fl oz) warm mineral water
1L (34 fl oz) olive oil

For the topping
150ml (5¼ fl oz) mild olive oil
4 medium onions, finely sliced
1 tbsp cream
5g (¼oz) Cabrales cheese (or any kind of blue cheese)
pinch of salt
2 organic eggs

1 Mix together the salt with the two types of flour in a large bowl, and slowly add the warm water.

2 Mix well until it forms a smooth dough and leave to rest for 6 hours.

3 Make the topping by putting the 150ml (5¼ fl oz) olive oil in a large frying pan and adding the onions. Fry them very gently over a low heat until they turn dark brown (this should take about two hours).

4 Divide the dough into small portions of about 20g (¾oz), and stretch them out into circles of about 9cm (3½in) in diameter.

5 Heat the 1L (34 fl oz) olive oil in a large, high-sided, heavy-bottomed saucepan.

6 Fry the *tortos* in the oil, turning them to ensure that they are evenly cooked. Remove from the oil when puffed up and golden, and drain on kitchen paper.

7 In a separate saucepan, heat the cream, Cabrales cheese and pinch of salt together until they melt, and add to the caramelised onion.

8 Put the onion mixture in a small frying pan. Break the two eggs into the pan, and stir briskly over a medium heat to make smooth, creamy scrambled eggs.

9 Put a thin topping of the scrambled egg mixture on top of each *torto* and serve.

PIXÍN CON TXANGURRO Y ALIOLI LIGERO

Monkfish with spider crab & light alioli

A marriage of Asturian and Basque cuisines, this rich dish of monkfish with flambéed spider crab showcases the best of both of them, says chef Guillermo Zabala.

Monkfish (or *pixín*, as it is known in Asturias) with a rich flambéed mix of spider crab and vegetables might be what passes for fusion in these parts. Part Asturian, part Basque, it's typical of the creations at Casa Zabala, a venerable old restaurant with a thoroughly modern outlook, located in a 17th -century building that once served duty as a hospital for pilgrims on the Camino de Santiago.

'There's a story behind this marriage of inspirations,' says chef Guillermo Zabala, 'A story that goes back two generations.' His great-grandfather was a Basque coastal skipper, he explains, who would bring wood and iron by boat to Gijón. On one of his trips, in 1923, when he was already widowed and close to retiring, he met and married a woman from Gijón and – despite not speaking a word of Spanish – decided to settle here and set up a restaurant.

'It was a slightly divey tavern at first,' explains Guillermo, 'But my great-grandfather started introducing Basque dishes, which we still serve to this day. Even the cuts he was familiar with were different. He taught local fishers about *ventresca*, the belly of the bonito, which was unheard of at the time, and is now a regular feature on menus all over Asturias. But it began right here.'

Many years later, the young Guillermo was working in the kitchens under the watchful 'and very impatient' eye of his mother. 'She was good,' he said, 'but her repertoire was limited. We just had a couple of starters, hardly any meat dishes, and a couple of desserts. I told her she should think about retiring but that I could take over, I could do it. I made a lot of mistakes along the way, but created a lot of successes too. Nowadays I can't imagine doing anything else. This is a job that gives you satisfaction like no other.'

Chef //
Guillermo Zabala
Location //
Casa Zabala, Gijón

PIXÍN CON TXANGURRO Y ALIOLI LIGERO

Monkfish with spider crab & light alioli

Serves 5

Preparation & cooking time 2hr

6 tbsp olive oil for frying
1 medium onion, finely diced
1 medium leek, finely diced
2 medium tomatoes, juiced in a blender
40ml (1½ fl oz) brandy
40ml (1½ fl oz) dry sherry
200g (7oz) crab meat (preferably spider crab)
5 x 200g (7oz) portions of monkfish

For the alioli
2 cloves of garlic, peeled
100ml (3½ fl oz) olive oil
35ml (1¼ fl oz) milk
1 tbsp parsley

1 Heat about 3tbsp of the olive oil in a large saucepan and gently sauté the onion, leek and tomatoes over a low heat for 10 minutes. Add the brandy, carefully set fire to the mix, and once the flame has gone out, add the sherry. Stir and leave for 20 minutes.

2 Add the crab meat, and cook for another 5 minutes.

3 Make the *alioli* by using a liquidiser to blend the garlic in the oil, and adding the milk very slowly. Finish off by adding the parsley.

4 Fry the monkfish in a dash of olive oil until golden on the outside and still juicy on the inside.

5 Arrange a spoonful of the crab meat and vegetable mixture on the plate, add a line of *alioli*, and place the monkfish on top.

Tip

If available, choose black monkfish, which has a lower water content and a better flavour and texture when cooked.

CARICO MONTAÑÉS
Bean stew

A classic of Cantabrian cuisine, carico montañés is given a deft touch at Jesús Sánchez Sainz's Michelin-starred restaurant in the coach house of a stunning 18th-century mansion.

The Spanish are passionate about their legumes, and dress them up in all kinds of ways. There is a whole genre – *platos de cuchara* ('spoon dishes') – to describe these unctuous plates of comfort food, which are easy to prepare, nutritious and filling. 'If there's one kind of food I could never give up it would be vegetables,' says Jesús Sánchez Sainz. 'If there was a utensil I could never give up it would be a spoon. The *carico* stew grants all my wishes.'

A red bean, with a small black mark, the *carico montañés* is peculiar to Cantabria, and is prized for both its taste and texture. According to Jesús, it has long been a mainstay of local cooking, along with corn, broad beans and chestnuts, and there are records of its use going back to the 17th century. 'Recipes based on legumes often use a lot of protein and animal fat,' he goes on, 'but there are some great exceptions in Spanish cooking – we have chickpea dishes, lentil stews or recipes with *pochas* (a young haricot bean), which are usually just cooked with a few vegetables.'

'It's important that the beans are not too old,' he adds. 'Ideally they shouldn't be more than a year, and I prefer the very small ones. I do a tasting with my producers every year to figure out the particular characteristics of that year's harvest. The beans shouldn't break up during the cooking process and the skin shouldn't be tough.'

This is a dish you can serve as a main course or as a side dish with meat. 'Many people serve it with the products of the *matanza* (an annual pig-slaughtering ceremony), but I prefer a meat-free version. Just a small starter, topped with some vegetables for different textures. But the bean is the thing.'

Chef //
Jesús Sánchez Sainz
Location //
Cenador de Amós,
Villaverde de Pontones

CARICO MONTAÑÉS
Bean stew

Serves 4

Preparation & cooking time 2hr, not including soaking beans

300g (10½oz) carico beans (try pinto beans as
    a substitute)
2 pinches of pimentón dulce (sweet paprika)
30g (1oz) red pepper
30g (1oz) green pepper
1 large whole onion, peeled
1 small tomato, peeled
1 clove of garlic, peeled
30g (1oz) pumpkin (optional), peeled
2 medium onions, peeled & finely chopped
75ml (2½ fl oz) extra virgin olive oil
pinch of salt, to taste

1 Wash the beans and put them to soak in plenty of cold water for 24 hours.

2 Put the beans and the water used to soak them, adding a little extra if necessary, in a large saucepan and add a pinch of paprika.

3 Chop the peppers, the large onion and the pumpkin (if used) into large chunks (so that they can easily be removed later), and add to the water with the tomato and garlic. Cook over a medium heat until it begins to boil.

4 When the water boils, skim off the froth to keep the broth clear, then lower the heat. Simmer for one hour with the saucepan lid on, and for another hour with the saucepan lid off.

5 Put the finely chopped onions in a frying pan and cook in olive oil on a very low heat for about an hour until translucent.

6 Add the fried onions to the beans, and add another pinch of paprika.

7 Remove most of the vegetable chunks, and blend them with a liquidiser, then add the resulting vegetable cream to the bean mixture. Season to taste.

PULPO A LA MUGARDESA
Octopus in a Mugardos style

*A refined modern
take on a sticky
fishers' stew
of octopus and
vegetables, so
revered in its town
of origin that there
is an annual day
to celebrate its
existence.*

Galicians take their seafood extremely seriously, but there are few dishes that have an entire feast day dedicated to them. The Fiesta del Pulpo de Mugardos takes place every July in the little town for which the dish is named at the mouth of the River Ferrol.

'This is a dish originally made by fishermen,' says Javier Montero, chef at O Tragaluz. 'Over time, they added potatoes, peas, onions, peppers and paprika, which they'd cook in the water left over from cooking the octopus. This is a dish that my mother showed me, it reminds me of her. She loved these kind of stews, and I still like to revisit these dishes, based on good quality ingredients and simplicity. They take me back to my childhood. In the restaurant I make them a little more elegant, give them a little drama. With this one we cover the dish and add some smoking thyme and take the cover off at the table so that the aromas of land and sea mingle.'

'We use local octopus, but as long as it is good quality, frozen is fine. In fact you should freeze octopus to make it more tender. It breaks down the fibres. The other thing you should do is dip the tentacles into the boiling water three times before plunging the entire thing in. It makes them less tough.'

Javier was born into a restaurant family – his mother was a cook, his father a pastry chef, and they owned various bars, restaurants and hotels. 'But I had no intention of being a chef, I trained as an architect. That's why so many of my dishes are stacked vertically,' he laughs. 'No, I got into this purely out of the pleasure it brings me.'

Chef //
Javier Montero
Location //
O Tragaluz, Santiago
de Compostela

PULPO A LA MUGARDESA

Octopus in a Mugardos style

Serves 6

Preparation & cooking time 1 hr 30 min

*2kg (4½lb) octopus, cleaned & chopped
   into chunks*
2L (3½pt) water
2 onions, finely chopped
2 red peppers, finely chopped
2 green peppers, finely chopped
150ml (5¼ fl oz) olive oil, plus 3 tbsp
70ml (2½ fl oz) white wine
1L (1¾pt) fish stock
5 potatoes, peeled & cut into chunks
handful of fresh thyme (optional)
100g (3½oz) peas (optional)
1 clove of garlic, chopped finely
1 tsp pimentón dulce (sweet paprika)

1 Put the octopus in a saucepan with 2L of boiling water and cook until tender (about 20–30 minutes). Reserve the water.

2 Pour 3 tbsp of olive oil in a large saucepan and gently sauté the onion with the red and green peppers until soft.

3 Add the cooked octopus, and the wine, and allow to reduce.

4 When the wine has reduced, add the fish stock, the potatoes, the thyme leaves, the peas (if using) and a few tbsp of the reserved water used to cook the octopus. Simmer for about 20 minutes, or until the potatoes are cooked.

5 In a separate frying pan, gently sauté the garlic until golden. Take off the heat, and allow to cool slightly before stirring in the paprika.

6 Add the garlic-paprika mixture to the stew.

5 Allow to rest for 5 minutes, and serve. Optionally, and if you have a large glass bowl, or similar, you can scorch the thyme and place it underneath with the octopus to let the smoke imbue the dish. Uncover it at the table.

VIEIRAS A LA GALLEGA
Galician-style scallops

The vieira a la gallega is more than just a tasty local delicacy; it is rich with symbolism, especially for the city of Santiago de Compostela and its pilgrims.

In Galicia the omniscient scallop shell holds a significance far beyond the merely gastronomic; it is the symbol of St James, patron saint of Spain, who holds a special importance in this region for his final resting place – the majestic cathedral in Santiago de Compostela. There is more than one story of how this came to be: some say that a drowned knight rescued and resuscitated by St James was covered in scallop shells, or that the boat that carried St James' remains back to Spain after his beheading by Herod Agrippa overturned and his body was washed ashore surrounded by scallops.

A further theory asserts that the grooves in the shell represent the different trails for the pilgrims following the Camino de Santiago. It is nowadays the official symbol of the route, and appears on posts all along it, and is attached to backpacks by pilgrims as a way of making their lofty intentions known. In days gone by they would also use the shell as a makeshift bowl. More prosaically, it has become the number one souvenir of the route.

A happy by-product of this demand is the tender, exquisite flesh of the molluscs themselves, eaten in abundance as *vieiras a la gallega* (scallops in a Galician style), smothered with onions and, occasionally, ham, and often covered with a crust of breadcrumbs. 'There are many dishes that we try to make our own,' says Gonzalo Abal Lobato, chef at O Dezaseis. 'But this is not one of them. A huge amount of our customers are pilgrims, since we're at the entrance to the old city and they make up a lot of our passing trade. This is the most typical dish we have in Galicia, and there's no reason to change it.'

Chef //
Gonzalo Abal Lobato
Location //
O Dezaseis, A Coruña

VIEIRAS A
LA GALLEGA
Galician-style scallops

Serves 6

Preparation & cooking time 30min

12 scallops
1½kg (3¼lb) onions, finely chopped
200ml (7 fl oz) olive oil
1 bay leaf
1 tsp pimentón dulce (sweet paprika)
100ml (3½ fl oz) white wine (preferably Albariño)

1 Pre-heat the oven to 200°C (390°F).

2 Carefully clean the scallops, ensuring that all the grit has been removed, and arrange in an oven-proof dish.

3 Gently fry the onion in the olive oil with the bay leaf in a covered frying pan until soft and translucent.

4 Add the paprika and then the wine, and allow to reduce.

5 Cover the scallops in the onion mixture, and cook in the oven for 7 minutes.

Tip

For a crusty topping, sprinkle some breadcrumbs over the onion before the dish goes in the oven. At O Dezaseis, they blend the fried onion in a food processor for a smoother taste.

PANTXINETA
Almond cream pastry

A triumph of Franco-Basque pastry-making, the pantxineta has its roots in WWI and the patronage of Spanish aristocracy, but is nowadays San Sebastián's favourite dessert.

Like its architecture, much of San Sebastián's gastronomy has been shaped both by its proximity to France and by its enduring popularity as a holiday resort with royalty and the ruling classes. At the beginning of the 20th century, WWI and its hardships meant that ingredients were limited, and creativity was as necessary as it was desirable, but it also meant that many French and Swiss citizens were stranded on this side of the border, and a great number of them sought work in restaurants and patisseries, and brought their own culinary influences. At the same time, San Sebastián continued to be a playground for the nobility, creating an enthusiastic market for the chefs' best efforts. And so it was that the *pantxineta* – a millefeuille with a rich custard centre, topped with slivers of almond – was born.

'The name was originally a bastardisation of the French *frangipane*,' says Patricio Fuentes, head chef at the San Sebastián Food cooking school. 'Which in itself came from an Italian called Cesare Frangipani, who created a perfume based on the scent of almonds that Louis XIII would wear on his gloves. The Basques would call it *frantxi-pani*, and from there it become *pantxineta*. It was made popular by Queen María Cristina and her court, but was eaten in homes throughout the region. Every family had its own recipe, especially for the custard, for which they used to use flour in place of cornstarch. The Basques have never had much of a tradition of pastry-making, but over time, this became the Basque dessert par excellence. In San Sebastián it's a classic. It's the one we turn to for fiestas and Christmas Day.'

Chef //
Patricio Fuentes
Location //
San Sebastián Food,
San Sebastián

PANTXINETA
Almond cream pastry

Serves 4

Preparation & cooking time 45min

For the pastry
250g (9oz) flour, plus extra for flouring
2 tsp salt
100ml (3½ fl oz) water
250g (9oz) butter, sliced & chilled

For the cream
3 egg yolks
60g (2oz) sugar
35g (1¼oz) cornstarch
600ml (1pt) milk
the peel of a large lemon (in one piece)
50g (1¾oz) almonds, sliced & lightly toasted,
  to serve

1 Preheat the oven to 200°C (390°F).

2 Put the flour in a bowl. Make a well in the centre, and add the salt and water. Mix well, and then knead until you get a smooth, elastic dough. Refrigerate the dough for a couple of hours.

3 Turn the chilled dough out on to a lightly floured board, and roll out into the rough shape of a cross. Put the slices of chilled butter in the centre of the cross, and fold in the 'arms' of the cross.

4 Roll out the dough into a square. Fold the top part down to the centre, then the bottom up to meet it. Roll out again into a square shape, and fold again as before. Repeat six times.

5 Roll out the dough to ½ cm (¼in) thickness and cut into preferred shape and size. Cook for about 20 minutes on a baking sheet/tray and lower the temperature to 190°C (375°F) if it begins to brown too quickly. Leave to cool.

6 Mix together the egg yolks, sugar and cornstarch.

7 Heat the milk with the lemon peel in a saucepan over a medium-high heat. Add the egg yolk mixture, stirring continuously to ensure it doesn't burn. Take out the peel, then remove the pan from the heat and allow the custard to cool.

8 Spoon the custard into the pastry cases and sprinkle with the sliced almonds. If desired, use a kitchen blowtorch to brown the top.

CREMA DE ARROZ CON LECHE REQUEMADA
Scorched rice pudding

The green rolling hills and steady rainfall of Spain's northwestern corner have made it the centre for dairy production, and the freshest milk imaginable goes into this classic rice pudding.

Housed in a 19th-century building that has variously served as a staging post, a cinema, a cider-house and a dance hall, Casa Gerardo has been functioning as a restaurant since 1882, always in the hands of the same family. Just outside Gijón, it is surrounded by rolling hills and the verdant pastureland for which Asturias is famous. The region is the epicentre for dairy production in Spain, and has its own protected breed of cows, the Asturian Valley cattle, known for the high quality of their meat and milk.

'We've been making this recipe here since the very beginning – first my great great grandfather, then my great grandfather, my grandfather, and now my father and me. It's changed from a humble *casa de comida* to something quite avant-garde, but we've always had a lot of time for the most traditional Asturian dishes, like the *fabada asturiana* (Spanish bean stew) or the *arroz con leche* (rice pudding),' says chef Marcos Morán.

The *arroz con leche* reflects its surrounding environment, and dairy products in these parts are spoken about with a sense of terroir. 'The *arroz* is a classic,' he says, 'but it's not about the rice, it's all about the milk. The milk should be raw – where raw milk is legal, and available – but if that's not possible, it should at least be as fresh as possible, and full cream, with a very high fat content,' he emphasises.

'It doesn't need much – just a touch of vanilla, a hint of cinnamon – but one of the things that makes this recipe unique is that, just before we take it out to the dining room, we sear the top with an iron, heated in the fire, and that caramelises the surface. That added bite just makes ours that little bit more special than the conventional version.'

Chef //
Marcos Morán
Location //
Casa Gerardo, Prendes

CREMA DE ARROZ CON LECHE REQUEMADA

Scorched rice pudding

Serves 6

Preparation & cooking time 1hr 30min

100g (3½oz) short-grain rice
200ml (⅓pt) water
½ cinnamon stick
½ vanilla pod
1.3L (2¼pt) fresh milk
50g (1¾oz) butter, cut into small pieces
pinch of salt
200g (7oz) sugar
extra sugar for caramelising

1 Heat the rice, water, cinnamon stick and vanilla pod in a pan over a low heat, stirring carefully to make sure it doesn't stick.

2 Cook until the rice forms a paste, then take off the heat and remove the cinnamon stick and vanilla pod.

3 Heat the milk in a separate, large pan. When it comes to the boil, add the rice paste, stirring frequently for an hour or so with a wooden spoon to make sure the rice doesn't stick.

4 When the mixture starts thickening (it's ready when you lift the spoon and there's an indentation in the mixture), slowly add the butter, and then take the pan off the heat.

5 Add the salt, and then slowly add the sugar. The mixture will thin out at first, but when it thickens up again, it is ready to serve.

6 Spoon the mixture into a large serving dish (could also be served in six ramekins).

7 Sprinkle a little more sugar evenly over the top of the mixture and caramelise with a blowtorch (or put under the grill for a few minutes until the sugar bubbles).

Tip

The rice pudding should be cooked on a plancha (hotplate) to ensure an even heat. Alternatively, it can be made on a gas ring, although ideally a diffuser should be used to make the heat even.

TARTA DE SANTIAGO
St James' cake

Moist but crumbly, nutty and sweet, the tarta de Santiago is easy to make and even easier to eat. Galician chef Koki García shares his version.

The *tarta de Santiago* is something of a mystery, given that Galicia is not really an almond-growing region, but recipes for it date back to the Middle Ages.

It was only a century ago, however, that the cake gained its distinctive cross, etched into the icing sugar, and it was then that it changed name from *torta real* (royal cake) to honour Galicia's patron saint. That this cake has gained so much popularity outside Spain probably comes down to the international presence on the Camino, and these days it's often chosen as the one that most represents Spanish desserts.

'I remember when I did the Camino de Santiago,' says Koki García, 'And the *tarta* was everywhere. I think it must have started out being popular on the walk for practical reasons, because it's fairly resilient, easy to carry in your pocket, and unlike most cakes is still good to eat after a couple of days. You could even eat it on the fourth or fifth day, so it's ideal for pilgrims.'

The *tarta de Santiago* is just one of the Galician specialities to come out of Mesón de Alberto, the restaurant founded by Koki's father in 1975. Photos of eminent patrons line the walls, including Pope John Paul II, who presumably can only have approved of this ecclesiastically named tart.

'It's pretty simple to make,' says Koki, 'There are no tricks – it's a recipe that's been used for centuries. You just need to follow the measures fairly closely, or it will be too dry or too liquid to cook properly. And test an almond before you buy – they shouldn't be too bitter.' Because of its unique texture, he recommends serving with 'something creamy, or liquid'. A fruit or chocolate sauce would go well, or a papally approved holy wine.

Chef //
Koki García
Location //
Mesón de Alberto, Lugo

TARTA DE SANTIAGO
St James' cake

Serves 6

Preparation & cooking time 1hr

250g (½lb) strong flour
125g (4½oz) butter
325g (¾lb) sugar
3 medium eggs
knob of butter, for greasing
250g (½lb) almonds (blanched)
zest of ½ a lemon
icing sugar, to serve

1 Preheat the oven to 180°C (350°F).

2 Mix the flour, the butter, 125g (4½oz) of the sugar, and one egg together to form the pastry. Let it rest for 20 minutes, then put into a 22cm- (8½in) diameter baking tin pre-greased with butter, and bake blind in the oven for 15 minutes.

3 Grind the almonds, and mix this almond meal with the remaining two eggs, rest of the sugar and the zest of half a lemon.

4 Put the almond mixture in the pastry case, and bake in the oven for 30 minutes.

5 When cooked, leave to cool, then decorate with a liberal dusting of icing sugar.

Tip

The tart is also commonly made without the pastry, just as a cake. With the pastry, it needs to be sufficiently moist, which is better achieved if you grind the almonds yourself – pre-ground almonds can be very dry. The St James' cross is easy to achieve by cutting the shape out of paper and placing on top before you liberally dust with icing sugar.

A slice of tarta de Santiago is often served with a small shot glass of sweet wine, such as a moscatel, which can be poured over the top.

ATLANTIC
OCEAN

Huelva

SEVILLE

CÁDIZ

El Puerto de
Santa María

Jerez

SPAIN

CÓRDOBA

Andalucía

Jaén

GRANADA

MÁLAGA

Strait of Gibraltar

Gibraltar (UK)

Ceuta (SPAIN)

MOROCCO

MEDITERRANEAN
SEA

ALMERÍA

Murcia

MURCIA

Cartagena

Southern
Spain

SOUTH SPAIN

In this archetypal Spanish region, dishes reflect not only the torrid climate, but its storied past. From bullfighting comes oxtail stew; from a historic coalition of sherry-makers and nuns come rich, eggy custards; from the Moorish invasion come battered lemon leaves and a smoky vegetable stew; and from devout Lenten rituals comes chickpeas with spinach.

GAZPACHO
Chilled tomato soup

Drunk from a glass with ice or topped with egg, vegetables and croutons and eaten with a spoon, this is the Spanish summer dish par excellence.

In the searing heat of a Seville summer, the inhabitants stay indoors and walk in the shadows. This is when the gazpacho comes into its own, and street-side stalls with vendors handing out iced glasses of this fragrant chilled soup pop up everywhere. Something of a proto-smoothie, gazpacho started life – as did so many of the cornerstones of Spanish cuisine – as a way for the workers to get a refreshing, nutritionally packed hit as they toiled in the fields under a punishing sun. It comes from the word *caspa*, meaning 'fragments' or 'leftovers' in the Mozarabic language, a dialect of Latin spoken in the areas of Spain under Moorish occupation. A close relation of *salmorejo* (see p239) and *ajoblanco* (see p227), it is these days eaten all over Spain.

Though it began, in the way of so many Spanish dishes, as a simple blend of day-old bread, oil, vinegar and water, it was in Seville that it was converted to a tomato soup, when the production of New World-imported fruit and vegetables was taken up with gusto in the *huertos* (vegetable gardens) of this region.

Nowadays the basic recipe is interpreted in any number of ways – for a while cherry or melon gazpacho had its moment, along with an array of deconstructed versions, hot versions and solid versions. At the Antigua Abacería de San Lorenzo, a quaint, rambling series of little snugs, wooden shelving groaning with jars of local produce and legs of cured Iberian ham, they serve it *como Díos manda* – 'as God intended'. 'It has everything,' says owner Ramón López de Tejada. 'It gives you minerals, vitamins, water. It cools you down in summer, and the bread makes it satisfying. It's easy to make. It's a meal in itself.'

Chef //
Gracia Nina
Location //
Antigua Abacería de San
Lorenzo, Seville

GAZPACHO
Chilled tomato soup

Serves 6

Preparation & cooking time 30min, not including chilling time

60g (2oz) day-old white bread
2kg (4½lb) plum tomatoes (add tsp sugar
  if your tomatoes are not particularly
  ripe/sweet)
½ green pepper, deseeded & chopped
100g (3½oz) cucumber, peeled & chopped
1 clove garlic
50ml (1¾ fl oz) sherry vinegar
200ml (7 fl oz) olive oil
pinch salt
300ml (10½ fl oz) water
olive oil, to serve
finely diced hard-boiled egg, to serve
diced serrano ham, to serve
peeled, finely diced cucumber, to serve
  (optional)
finely diced spring onions, to serve
  (optional)
finely diced green pepper, to serve (optional)
croutons, to serve (optional)

1 Trim crusts from the bread, and place under the grill at a low heat to dry out.

2 Blend the bread in a liquidiser to make rough breadcrumbs.

3 Place the tomatoes, pepper, cucumber, breadcrumbs, garlic, vinegar, olive oil and salt in the liquidiser. Add half of the water and blend. Continue to add more water slowly until the soup reaches the desired consistency.

4 Cover and chill for 2 hours.

5 Serve topped with a drizzle of olive oil, and the traditional garnish of chopped boiled egg and ham. Optional garnishes include diced cucumber, spring onions, green pepper and croutons.

Tip

If you are making this soup in advance, remember that the garlic flavour will intensify the longer it is kept. Halve the quantity of garlic if you are serving it more than 24 hours after making it.

SOLDADITOS DE PAVÍA
Little soldiers of Pavía

A steady stream of crunchy, fluffy cod fritters, from a recipe passed down through seven generations, is churned out of the kitchen to meet demand at Seville's most evocative bar.

The Virgin Mary looks wistfully down on a burnished wooden bar, glistening haunches of ham hang from the beams, ancient tiles line the walls, and the decades of nicotine have done little to diminish the charm of the yellowing wooden tracery adorning the floor-to-ceiling shelves. This is El Rinconcillo, a tiny, untouched corned of old Seville that threw open its doors as a bodega and grocery shop in 1670 and has barely known a quiet moment since.

In 1858, the de Rueda family turned it into a modest restaurant and tapas bar, and Javier de Rueda, who runs El Rinconcillo today, is of the seventh generation of that same family. 'We still serve many of the same dishes,' he says. 'We can't be sure, but we think the *soldaditos de Pavía* have been made here since the beginning of the 19th century.' The whimsical name of these crispy, battered strips of cod is shrouded in mystery. Some say it harks back to the Battle of Pavía in 1525, a decisive victory for Charles V, Holy Roman Emperor, in winning back parts of Spain from the French. The theory goes that the *soldaditos* were named for the colour of the Spanish troops' uniform, which was yellow with red stripes, and in fact the cod was once served with strips of red pepper.

'They also say that it comes from General Pavía in the 19th century, whose soldiers had so little to eat that they would fry flour and water, and it was a few years later that cod was added,' says Javier. 'In those days cod was cheap and plentiful. So many of these dishes just started as a way of filling the stomach. These days it's one of our most popular tapas.'

Chef //
Daniel Toscano Sotelo
Location //
El Rinconcillo, Seville

SOLDADITOS DE PAVÍA
Soldiers of Pavía

Serves 4

Preparation & cooking time 2hr, not including soaking chickpeas/desalting cod

300g (10½ oz) salt cod fillet (soaked for 24 hours)
100g (3½oz) chickpeas (soaked overnight)
1L (1¾pt) water for cooking the chickpeas
100g (3½oz) flour
100g (3½oz) chickpea flour
8 eggs
4 cloves of garlic, chopped finely
1 onion, chopped finely
100ml (3½ fl oz) beer
100ml (3½ fl oz) water
salt & pepper, to taste
200ml (7 fl oz) extra virgin olive oil for frying
spinach leaves, to serve

1 Soak the salt cod for 24 hours to remove the salt, changing the water three or four times before rinsing with cold water at the end.

2 Soak the chickpeas in cold water overnight.

3 Put the chickpeas in a saucepan, cover with 1L (1¾pt) of water and bring to the boil. Then simmer for approximately 1 hour and 30 minutes or until the chickpeas are tender.

4 Puree the chickpeas in a blender.

5 Mix the flour, chickpea flour and eggs in a large bowl. Add the garlic, onion, beer, 100ml (3½ fl oz) of water, salt and pepper to taste, then the chickpea puree, and mix with a spatula until it forms a paste.

6 Heat the olive oil in a heavy-based, high-sided saucepan.

7 Dip the cod strips in the chickpea batter, and then fry in the hot olive oil until golden.

8 Dry the fried cod strips on kitchen paper and serve on a bed of spinach leaves.

AJOBLANCO DE ANACARDO
Chilled cashew soup

This white creamy soup, kissing cousin of gazpacho, has its roots in Moorish Spain and goes back hundreds of years. Jota Leirós gives it the tiniest of tweaks.

La Chalá ('the crazy woman') is a restaurant that comes with its own subtitle – 'Confessions of a modern grandmother' – a playful statement of intent that sums up its irreverent approach to reinventing the classics. For all its funky reggae, the AstroTurf pinned to the wall, the goldfish in jam jars, mismatched furniture and splashy, cartoonish elements, however, this is a place that is deadly serious about its food and wine. This is something that is evident from a quick glance at the menu, which takes time-honoured favourites and gives them a new lick of paint.

'I've been cooking since I was nine,' says Jota Leirós, La Chalá's chef. 'I didn't like football, I liked cooking. Mostly I learnt from my mother, who cooks really well, but we also had a cook who helped out and she was Muslim, so a lot of my influences come from that.' The *ajoblanco*, too, owes a lot to Muslim influence, and it was the Moorish occupation, when this area was Al-Andalus, that made the use of almonds and other nuts so popular in local cooking.

'Usually *ajoblanco* is made with almonds,' says Jota Leirós. 'But for me the classic version is a bit dense, so I make it with cashews. It makes it slightly sweeter too. It's been around for 500 years or so, or at least a garlic, bread and nut soup has existed since then, occasionally made with chestnuts or acorns, but mostly with almonds. It comes from Córdoba originally and all the areas near here where almonds grow. You could also make it with pistachios or pine nuts. It's very versatile and very easy to make – you don't want too much of it because it's very rich and filling, but if you add vinegar to whatever's left over, it makes a great dressing for salad.'

Chef //
Jota Leirós
Location //
La Chalá, Seville

AJOBLANCO DE ANACARDO
Chilled cashew soup

Serves 6

Preparation & cooking time 30min

100g (3½oz) white bread
300ml (½pt) full cream milk
100ml (3½ fl oz) water, plus extra for liquidising
(optional)
200g (7oz) roasted cashews
1 clove of garlic, peeled
100ml (3½ fl oz) extra virgin olive oil
150ml (5¼ fl oz) sunflower oil
3 tbsp honey
1 tbsp sherry vinegar
salt, to taste
garnishes (see Tip)

1 Pre-soak the bread in the milk and water.

2 Put the cashews, garlic, and the bread with milk and water in a liquidiser and blend.

3 While liquidising, slowly add the olive and sunflower oils. Add water as necessary so that the soup doesn't get too thick, then add the honey, vinegar and salt, blending well.

4 Chill in the fridge for 30 minutes to an hour.

5 Garnish and serve.

Tip

There's no end to the things that can be used to garnish ajoblanco, but you could try avocado, mango, prawns, mojama (cured tuna) or herring roe.

GARBANZOS CON ESPINACAS
Chickpeas with spinach

A small earthenware dish of lightly spiced chickpeas and spinach is the sevillano tapa snack of choice, evoking the city's profoundly sombre Catholic rituals, as well as its colourful Moorish past.

The smell of incense wafts out into the street. Not, perhaps, the conventional way to lure passers-by into a tapas bar, but then again Casa Ricardo is no ordinary tapas bar. It is a shrine to the city's deepest religious traditions, to Semana Santa (Holy Week) and the slow processions that fill its streets during that time. These processions are led by the *cofradías*, the brotherhoods, in their strange penitential robes and poined hoods, as they carry crosses and bear aloft statues of the Virgin.

Every inch of the walls at Casa Ricardo is covered with memorabilia of processions past, from photos of the *cofradías* and effigies of the various virgins to the knotted emblems worn on the robes. 'When my father took over the bar it was just four white walls,' says Ricardo Núñez Romero, the current owner. 'My mother was horrified with what he did, because this kind of thing just didn't exist back then. She said, "this isn't a bar, this is a museum." She didn't think anyone would come.'

The tapas, too, pay homage to the oldest local rituals. And this dish is thought to be a derivation of *potaje* (stew) *de vigilia* (vigil; the eve of a holy day), which was eaten on each Friday of lent and during the whole of Semana Santa. 'To make it the traditional way, you should really crush the ingredients in a wooden bowl,' says Ricardo. 'That's how my grandmother would have done it.'

Either way, it is one of Seville's most tasty tapas, and an absolute godsend to vegetarians, who otherwise struggle around these parts. Thick and filling, the chickpeas are given a smoky flavour from the paprika, while the cumin hints at the Moorish legacy, as is so typical in Andalucían cooking.

Chef //
Ricardo Núñez Romero
Location //
Casa Ricardo, Seville

GARBANZOS CON ESPINACAS
Chickpeas with spinach

Serves 4

Preparation & cooking time 2hr, including cooking chickpeas

2L (3½pt) water
2 bay leaves
300g (10½ oz) chickpeas, pre-soaked
3 tbsp olive oil
6 baguette slices
3 cloves of garlic, peeled
½ tbsp cumin seeds
½ tbsp pimentón dulce (sweet paprika)
pinch of salt
400g (14oz) spinach, washed & finely chopped

1 Boil the water in a large saucepan, and add the bay leaves and pre-soaked chickpeas. Cook for approximately 90 minutes or until the chickpeas are tender.

2 Drain the chickpeas and set aside.

3 Heat the olive oil in a large frying pan, and toast the baguette slices and garlic cloves over a medium heat. When the bread and the cloves are golden, remove from the frying pan and reserve the oil.

4 Use a mortar and pestle to crush two of the bread slices with the browned garlic cloves, the cumin seeds, paprika, and a pinch of salt.

5 Put the mixture in the frying pan with the oil used to cook the bread slices, and sauté gently for a minute or two. Add the cooked chickpeas and the spinach, and heat through, stirring continuously to ensure it doesn't stick.

6 Serve hot, garnished with a slice of toasted baguette.

Tip

To save time, you could also use a jar of chickpeas.

TORTILLITA DE CAMARONES
Shrimp fritters

El Puerto de Santa María is a quintessentially Andalucían town that makes good use of its maritime bounty. Crunchy shrimp fritters and a glass of sherry are the perfect introduction.

Fernando Córdoba is something of a custodian of Andalucía's gastronomy, determined to stay out of the spotlight but nonetheless respected by chefs from all over the country. He now runs various concerns in the region, but his flagship is the elegant El Faro de El Puerto, a converted light-filled villa with a kitchen garden and an impressive wine cellar. Among the 400 labels on offer, he keeps a huge selection of sherries, made mostly in nearby Jerez, and he delights in the seafood and sherry pairings that are at the heart of the local maritime cuisine.

A crisp, dry manzanilla or fino goes particularly well with his legendary *tortillitas* (fritters), so fine that, balanced on their side, the fritters glow with a golden hue as the sunlight streams through. 'This is the signature dish of the restaurant,' says Fernando. 'All the ingredients are local, including the *camarones*, which are tiny estuarine shrimps from the Bay of Cádiz. Round here there's a lot of salt-water marshland full of fish, which breed naturally and taste nothing like the farmed fish. There's an abundance of these *camarones*, which we get delivered almost every day, freshly caught.'

The batter was traditionally made with chickpea flour, which started during the Siege of Cádiz when the wheat stocks ran low. 'But these days,' says Fernando, 'we make ours with regular flour, which makes the fritters lighter, more crunchy and less oily. The only ingredients are scallions, shrimps, parsley, flour, salt and water.'

Fernando picks up what looks like leafy green algae. 'In El Faro we add sea lettuce, because so much of it grows around here, and it gives it a little marine touch, with just a hint of the sea. We put all this together to make the batter, which is at once very simple and very complicated. The texture of the mixture is really important, as is the temperature of the oil, which needs to be really hot. It takes a bit of practice.'

Chef //
Fernando Córdoba
Location //
El Faro de El Puerto, El Puerto de Santa María

TORTILLITA
DE CAMARONES
Shrimp fritters

Serves 4–6

Preparation & cooking time 30min

100g (3½oz) flour
350–400ml (12–14 fl oz) water
pinch of salt
20g (¾oz) sea lettuce or other seaweed (optional)
100g (3½oz) shrimp
20g (¾oz) scallions (or spring onions if unavailable), finely chopped
15g (½oz) parsley, finely chopped
1L (34 fl oz) olive oil for frying

1 Mix the flour, water and salt in a bowl to make a batter.

2 Add the sea lettuce, shrimp, scallions and parsley. Ensure the batter isn't too runny. If it is, add a little more flour.

3 Heat about 2cm (1in) of oil in a large frying pan, until very hot. Add the batter by the spoonful. When the fritters are cooked on one side, flip them over to cook on the other side.

4 Remove the fritters from the pan, carefully draining off excess oil, and serve immediately.

Tip

In the traditional recipe, very small estuarine prawns are used, and eaten whole.
These can be substituted with very small shrimp, but you may need to shell and remove the heads.

SALMOREJO
Thick tomato soup

The self-appointed ambassador for salmorejo, Juanjo Ruiz has turned this chilled, nourishing soup into an art form at his stall in the graceful 19th-century wrought-iron Mercado Victoria.

A thick, emulsified, soup, *salmorejo* is seen as something of a country cousin to the refined and light gazpacho, with which it has much in common. Its roots can be traced back to ancient times and there is evidence of 'bread soup' having existed not only in early Iberian settlements, but also further afield, in Mesopotamia.

In those days, and for many centuries to come, it would not involve much more than flour, or bread, garlic, salt and water. In Roman times, this was known as *puls*, and was adapted according to which vegetables were in season. The noble classes would add eggs and cheese, or sweeten it with honey and eat it like a dessert. Also related was the *posca*, a drink of water, salt and vinegar, often flavoured with rosemary and other herbs, which Roman soldiers would carry in their canteens.

'It was the isotonic drink of its day!' says Juanjo Ruiz, who has worked with archaeologists and historians to investigate where exactly the *salmorejo* came from. 'They would use their helmets as a mortar to grind up the bread and garlic, add some of the *posca* from their canteens and that's where it all began.'

Juanjo is passionate about his subject, and can quote scientific and medical studies that show how the act of blending the vegetables does part of the body's digestive work, and has beneficial effects on patients with cardiovascular problems. It was this fascination that led him to open La Salmoreteca in Córdoba's gastro-market, the Mercado Victoria. Here he turns out an unimaginable variety of *salmorejos*, from red curry to beetroot, from Mexican to white chocolate. It's the classic recipe he comes back to time and again, however. But why do it by hand? What does it add?

'It's more romantic,' he grins.

Chef //
Juanjo Ruiz
Location //
La Salmoreteca, Córdoba

SALMOREJO
Thick tomato soup

Serves 4

Preparation & cooking time 1hr

For the classic salmorejo
1 tsp fleur de sel (French sea salt)
3 cloves of garlic, peeled
100ml (3½ fl oz) extra virgin olive oil
135g (4¾oz) breadcrumbs
700g (1½lb) ripe plum tomatoes, peeled
  & chopped
slivers of cured ham, to serve
finely chopped boiled egg, to serve

For the salmorejo with squid ink
3 sheets dried nori, crumbled
1 tbsp squid ink
salt & pepper, to taste
fried onion/fried chunks of octopus/
  prawns, to serve

For the classic salmorejo

1 Put the salt in a large mortar or wooden salad bowl, and add the garlic and just a drop of olive oil. Grind with the pestle into a paste.

2 Add the breadcrumbs (pre-moistening them can make them easier to blend), and continue to grind until you have a smooth paste.

3 Add the tomatoes, using the pestle to attain a smooth consistency. Season to taste, and add more olive oil if necessary.

4 Serve chilled, drizzled with olive oil, and topped with the chopped ham and boiled egg.

For the salmorejo with squid ink

1 For a serving variation, make salmorejo as per the classic recipe above, adding the crumbled nori sheets with the tomatoes.

2 Stir in the squid ink and season to taste.

3 Serve chilled, and topped with the fried onion, octopus or prawns.

Tip

This is best in small portions and looks dramatic presented in an oyster shell, but ramekins would serve just as well.

RABO DE TORO ESTOFADO
Braised oxtail

A rich, hearty stew originating in a time when women would wait outside the bullrings for the tails, ears, offal and other cuts that would be rejected by butchers.

'This is the classic Córdoba dish, along with *salmorejo*,' (p239) says Juan Gutiérrez, head chef at Bodegas Campos. 'It's hard to find a restaurant round here that doesn't serve those two. It's tied in with *la vida taurina*, the bullfighting life, which is such a big part of Andalucían culture.' Close by is the *barrio* of Santa Marina, which was once famous for its abattoir, and also for the great bullfighters that it produced. Pepe Campos, whose grandfather founded the restaurant, explains, 'My uncle had lots of friends who were bullfighters, artists and so on, and we used to have lots of parties. This culture is a very inclusive one.'

Opened in 1908 as a bodega, where wine was stored and made, Bodegas Campos didn't become a fully fledged restaurant until 1980. 'After a particularly harsh year for vineyards and wine production,' says Pepe, 'we were forced to change direction, and we started serving food to our customers. The philosophy is traditional cooking, but "refreshed" a little.' The restaurant is often described as a living museum, a labyrinth of elegant dining rooms around shady courtyards and patios fragrant with jasmine. Its rambling nature stems from its origins – it started out as a modestly sized affair, but grew to incorporate more and more of the neighbouring buildings, among them an entire convent.

For over a century now, it has been a social hub for a certain circle of *cordobés* society, in which bullfighters would hang out with nobility, and writers and artists would rub shoulders with politicians and travelling guitarists. Many of its dining rooms encapsulate a particular aspect of the *solera* – a word that encapsulates character, pedigree and tradition – that has shaped the restaurant. 'There is one *sala* dedicated to flamenco,' says Pepe. 'Others to wine, fiestas, poets and, of course, bulls.'

Chef //
Juan Gutiérrez Moreno
Location //
Bodegas Campos, Córdoba

RABO DE
TORO ESTOFADO
Braised oxtail

Serves 4–6

Preparation & cooking time 4hr 30min

2kg (4½lb) oxtail, cut into chunks
75ml (2½ fl oz) olive oil
4 cloves of garlic, peeled & sliced
250g (½lb) onion, finely diced
250g (½lb) carrots, finely chopped
1 tsp black peppercorns
1 tsp cloves
150ml (5¼ fl oz) red wine
150ml (5¼ fl oz) white wine
2L (3½pt) beef stock
oloroso or amontillado sherry,
  to serve
1 tsp salt, to taste

1 Soak the oxtail in iced water for 10 minutes to remove any impurities (this means you won't have to skim the stew later). Remove and drain on kitchen paper.

2 Heat the olive oil in a large saucepan. Add the garlic, onion, carrots, peppercorns and cloves, and cook slowly until soft and caramelised.

3 Roast the chopped oxtail in a preheated oven at 220°C (430°F) for 20 minutes, then add to the vegetable mix in the saucepan.

4 Pour in the red and white wine, and simmer until the wine has reduced by half.

5 Add the stock, bring to the boil, put a lid on the saucepan, and then reduce the heat. Simmer gently until the meat is tender (approximately 3½–4 hours).

6 Season with salt, and serve accompanied by a glass of oloroso or amontillado sherry.

Note

For a variation on this recipe, you can debone the oxtail by hand, and press the meat into a patty. Top with creamed potato, and serve.

ALBORONÍA Y VINAGRETA DE MISO Y MIEL CON ATÚN

Braised vegetables with miso & honey dressing & tuna

Like so many Andalucían dishes, this one has its roots in Moorish Spain and combines the flavours of both cultures. Here, appropriately, it is served in a former souk.

There are variations on what might elsewhere be called ratatouille all over Spain. Catalunya has its *samfaina*, Castilla La Mancha has *pisto manchego* and the Balearic Islands have *tumbet* (p57), to name but a few. The earliest example, however, from which all others are said to have developed, is *alboronía*, the Andalucían rendering. As with so many Spanish dishes, this one has its origins in the Arab occupation of the region, and is said to have been named after the Princess Al-Buran for her wedding to the caliph Al-Mamun in 882, and was originally known as *alburaniya*. Gradually its popularity spread from Andalucía throughout the whole country, by which time the discoveries from the New World meant the addition of tomatoes and peppers.

It's appropriate then, that the little tapas restaurant named after the dish is located in Jerez's former *zoco* (souk). Set on a hill slightly apart from the rest of the old town, this cluster of buildings, with a wooden gallery looking down on a central leafy courtyard, has served variously as stables, a slaughterhouse and a meat market over the centuries, and has now been cleaned up by the council and restored to a place where craftspeople can sell their wares.

The courtyard serves as the terrace to the Alboronía restaurant, where Adelina Pandelet and Víctor Marín meld the flavours and dishes of the *zoco's* romantic past with its vibrant Andalucían present. Evocative aromas float from their tiny kitchen, where croquettes rub shoulders with tagine, and lamb is cooked with honey and saffron. 'The menu is short and changes frequently,' says Víctor, 'but the *alboronía* is a favourite dish, and something of a mainstay.' The terrace also hosts live music on occasional balmy evenings, as it did, no doubt, 900 years ago.

Chef //
Adelina Pandelet
Location //
Alboronía, Jerez
de la Frontera

ALBORONÍA Y VINAGRETA DE MISO Y MIEL CON ATÚN

*Braised vegetables with miso &
honey dressing & tuna*

Serves 4

Preparation & cooking time 1hr 30min

For the alboronía
2 medium aubergines (eggplant)
175g (6oz) pumpkin
1 courgette (zucchini)
1 onion
3 cloves of garlic
1 small green pepper
3 tbsp extra virgin olive oil
3 tbsp tomate frito (see p264)
salt, to taste

For the miso & honey dressing
150ml (5¼ fl oz) water
2½ tsp dashi
2 tsp miso paste
3 tbsp soy sauce
9 tbsp sunflower oil
2 tsp honey

For the tuna
3 tbsp extra virgin olive oil
4 x 100g (3½oz) portions of tuna
sesame seeds, to garnish
paprika oil, to garnish (see Tip)

1 Peel and finely chop the aubergines (eggplant), pumpkin, courgette (zucchini), onion, garlic and pepper.

2 Heat 3 tbsp of extra virgin olive oil in a large saucepan and gently fry the garlic. Add the onion, and soften. Then add the pepper, followed by the *tomate frito*, and stir. Then add the pumpkin, aubergines and courgette.

3 Add salt to taste, put a lid on the saucepan, and continue to cook over a low heat for about 30 minutes, or until the pumpkin is tender.

4 To make the dressing, boil the water in a saucepan. Turn off the heat, add the dashi and let it dissolve. Then add the miso and mix until it forms an emulsion. Add the rest of the dressing ingredients and beat thoroughly.

5 Heat another 3 tbsp of olive oil in a frying pan and sear the tuna on both sides until cooked (about 4–5 minutes).

6 To serve, form the *alboronía* into patties and arrange on the plate. Then pour over the dressing, and place the tuna on top. Sprinkle over some sesame seeds and drizzle with paprika oil.

Tip

To make paprika oil, mix 1 tbsp paprika in a frying pan with 180ml (6½ fl oz) olive oil, stir over medium heat for a few minutes until completely dissolved and strain through fine colander or filter paper.

CREMA DE POLEÁ CON ESTOFADO DE PIÑA Y JALEA DE VINO DULCE

Spiced cream with caramelised pineapple & sherry jelly

In the hands of accomplished pastelero (pastry cook) Manu Jara, the humble poleá has come a very long way from its roots as pre-Roman gruel.

Born in France to Spanish parents, Manu Jara did not set out to be a pastry chef. 'I was studying as a chef in France, and we had to do different manual assignments each week – roasting, decorating, and so on – and then it came to baking. I couldn't believe how much you could do with four ingredients! As long as you mixed and cooked them properly, you could create something sublime. It was a revelation.' After a long stint in some of the finest kitchens of Madrid, Manu came to Seville to set up a patisserie and cooking school. 'I love the city, and there's a lack of this kind of cooking here, so it was a great opportunity.'

He set up in a glorious old grocer's shop in Triana, a traditionally *gitano* neighbourhood on the west bank of the Guadalquivir river. The tiled floors, baroque counter and floor-to-ceiling carved wooden shelves have all been preserved, and the trays of pastries, tarts and mini-desserts also hark back to a bygone age.

'We want to bring back the things that the *trianeros* loved,' he says. 'But with the finest ingredients. The *poleá* has been around for as long as humanity, and is based simply on flour, water and oil. Instead of water we use milk, and we add it to a roux made from the olive oil and flour. With the arrival of the Arabs, the gastronomy of the area changed – there was honey, there were almonds and so on – and so we spice the milk with aniseed and citrus fruits to reflect that. I should admit that the original recipe just calls for oil, but, like the good Frenchman that I am, I do sneak a little butter in there.'

Chef //
Manu Jara
Location //
Manu Jara, Seville

CREMA DE POLEÁ CON ESTOFADO DE PIÑA Y JALEA DE VINO DULCE

Spiced cream with caramelised pineapple & sherry jelly

Serves 6

Preparation & cooking time 1hr

For the poleá

140g (5oz) sugar
2 heaped tsp aniseed seeds
1 orange rind (in one strip)
1 lemon rind (in one strip)
3 sticks of cinnamon
700ml (1¼pt) milk
15g (½oz) butter
35ml (1¼ fl oz) olive oil
50g (1¾oz) flour
70ml (2½ fl oz) olive oil (optional)

For the caramelised pineapple

80g (3oz) sugar
½ vanilla pod, split & de-seeded
250g (9oz) pineapple, chopped into
  small cubes

For the brioche croutons

2 thick slices of brioche, frozen
knob of butter

For the poleá

1 Put the sugar, aniseed, orange and lemon rind and cinnamon sticks in a saucepan with the milk, and bring to the boil. Remove from the heat, cover, and leave to infuse for 10 minutes. Then strain into a bowl.

2 Melt the butter with the olive oil in a saucepan, then stir in the flour gradually to make a roux.

3 Slowly add the spiced milk to the roux, and continue to stir until you get a smooth cream.

4 A little olive oil can be added at the end if required.

For the caramelised pineapple

1 Make a dry caramel by pouring sugar slowly and evenly into a heavy-bottomed saucepan, stirring gently over a low heat.

2 Add the vanilla pod and the beans, and continue to stir until all the sugar has melted to form the caramel.

3 Stir in the cubed pineapple until coated with the caramel.

For the brioche croutons

1 Cut off crusts, then cube the brioche.

2 Fry in a pan with a knob of hot butter until golden and drain on kitchen paper.

For the sherry jelly

200ml (6¾ fl oz) Pedro Ximénez
(see Note)
½ vanilla pod
200g (7oz) sugar
2 leaves of gelatine, soaked in cold water

For the decorations (optional)

salt flakes
tiny mint leaves
meringue drops

Note

Manu Jara used a sherry made
with the local Pedro Ximénez
grape for this dessert, but you
could substitute Amontillado
sherry, or a similar fortified wine.

For the sherry jelly

1 Warm the sherry in a saucepan with the vanilla pod and the sugar, and bring to the boil, then simmer for about 5 minutes.

2 Add the gelatine and stir.

3 Leave to cool.

Presentation

1 Arrange cubes of the caramelised pineapple at the bottom of each serving dish (a small jam jar is ideal, but a ramekin could serve).

2 Put the *poleá* into a piping bag, and squeeze over the pineapple. Chill for 30 minutes, or until set.

3 Pour the sherry jelly (at room temperature) over the back of a spoon on to the *poleá*.

4 Cool in the fridge for 20 minutes, then scatter over the brioche croutons, and some decorations if you wish: salt flakes, tiny mint leaves and/or meringue drops.

TOCINO DE CIELO
Heavenly 'lard'

The curious backstory of this impossibly rich dessert (with an equally unusual name) goes back to the Phoenicians and ends behind the walls of the closed convents of medieval (and, indeed, modern) Spain.

The romantic Spanish archetype, Jerez ticks all the boxes. Scarlet geraniums tumble from balconies gracing whitewashed houses that flank narrow cobbled streets. The plaintive strains of flamenco fill the air, and the bars line their walls with curling, nicotine-stained posters advertising bullfights. Above all, there is sherry. The very word 'sherry' is an anglicisation of 'Jerez' (no such label exists in Spanish). Great oak sherry barrels are used for decoration, for bar tables and to sit on. Huge bodegas tower above the shady plazas and bear familiar names – Tio Pepe, Sandeman, González Byass.

The Phoenicians introduced winemaking to the region in 1100 BC, a mantle that was taken up by the Moors, and subsequently – once these lands were recaptured – the Spanish. By the 14th century, the sherry-making industry was a vast concern, and with it brought a very specific kind of industrial waste in the shape of tons and tons of egg yolks. The whites were used to clarify the wine, and the yolks would be discarded until the bodegas moved to donate them to local convents, where the nuns would turn them into confectionery and desserts. One of the most popular was *tocino de cielo*, roughly translated as 'heavenly lard', for the texture and marbled appearance when the syrup runs through the cracks.

By this time wine was being made all over Spain, and the practice became countrywide. The *tocino* from Jerez is still considered somewhat sacred, however, and the local authorities have applied to give it PGI (Protected Geographical Indication), which is pending an EU decision. Within Jerez itself, La Carboná is considered the best place to try it, and when Parisian superchef Iñaki Aitzpitarte wanted to introduce the dish to his legendary restaurant Le Chateaubriand, it was here that he came to see just how it should be done.

Chef //
Javier Muñoz
Location //
La Carboná,
Jerez de la Frontera

TOCINO DE CIELO
Heavenly 'lard'

Serves 4–6

Preparation & cooking time 1hr

Ingredients:
10 egg yolks
½ white of one egg
125g (4½oz) plus 250g (8¾oz) sugar
125ml (4½ fl oz) water
sherry/sweet wine, to serve

1 Whisk together the egg yolks with the egg white.

2 Spread 125g (4½oz) of sugar evenly in the bottom of a heavy-based saucepan over a low heat. Allow to caramelise without stirring, and remove from the heat when it becomes a dark caramel sauce.

3 Boil the water in a saucepan with 250g (8¾oz) of sugar until a syrup forms.

4 Coat the bottom of a baking dish with the caramel from step 2.

5 Whisk the syrup from step 3 and the beaten eggs together.

6 Carefully pour the egg mixture through a sieve into a baking dish.

7 Create a bain-marie using a bigger dish half-filled with water and bringing it to a medium heat. Place the dish with the eggs inside it – ensuring it doesn't touch the bottom by resting on something heatproof – for 20 minutes, and then leave to cool for 10 minutes.

8 Cover and leave in the fridge for 5 hours or so to set.

9 Serve with sherry or sweet wine.

PAPAJAROTES
Fried lemon leaves

One of the more weird and wonderful desserts that Spain has to offer is the paparajote, a leavened batter given an aromatic touch from the leaf of a lemon tree.

At first glance, there is little to explain Murcia's moniker of *la huerta de Europa* (Europe's vegetable garden). Hot, dusty and dry by nature, this doesn't seem like a region that could possibly be exporting fruit and vegetables to the rest of the country and beyond. Thanks to the Arab invasion in the 8th century, however, Murcia has an incredibly sophisticated system of *acequías* (water conduits), that draw water from the rivers and irrigate vast swathes of land, creating verdant valleys and orchards.

The Moors not only introduced their skills and their infrastructure, they also brought with them fruit and vegetables of every description. Among these were orange and lemon trees, which now proliferate along the Murcian and Valencian coasts. Nothing is wasted, and lemon leaves are used to flavour all manner of dishes, both sweet and savoury. The most common, however, is the *paparajote*, which has been eaten as a cheap, easily made dessert for centuries. This curious snack comprises, simply, the leaves of a lemon (or orange) tree, coated in batter, fried and eaten – while piping hot – by scraping the sugar and cinnamon coated batter off the leaf between your front teeth, as one might scrape the flesh from an artichoke petal. It's important not to eat the leaf, which is there to impart a fragrant hint of citrus, nothing more.

'There's not much to it,' says Miguel López Hernández, who has been making them at La Pequeña Taberna since 1980, when he was a mere 16 years old. 'Except that you have to use fresh leaves, they have a much better aroma. *Paparajotes* are very easy to make, but to do them really well, and to keep the batter from sliding off the leaf, you have to do it with patience and with love. That's the only secret. Love.'

Chef //
Miguel López Hernández
Location //
La Pequeña Taberna, Murcia

PAPAJAROTES
Fried lemon leaves

Serves 6

Preparation & cooking time 1hr

6 eggs
500ml (17½ fl oz) milk
a pinch of salt
100g (3½oz) sugar
1 sachet (15g/½oz) baking powder
zest of 1 lemon
500g (1lb) flour
approx 18–24 lemon tree leaves,
    thoroughly washed
1L (35 fl oz) olive oil for frying
50g (1¾oz) icing sugar
2 tsp ground cinnamon

1 Make the batter by beating the eggs in a large bowl and adding the milk, salt, sugar, baking powder and lemon zest. Add the flour slowly, while continuing to mix, to ensure that the batter doesn't get too thick. (It should be just thick enough to coat the leaves.)

2 Dip the lemon-tree leaves in the batter, making sure they are evenly coated on both sides.

3 Heat the olive oil in a large saucepan, and fry the leaves until golden all over.

4 Remove from the oil and drain on kitchen paper.

5 Dust with icing sugar and cinnamon, and serve.

BASIC RECIPES

TOMATE FRITO

Ingredients
1 small onion, peeled & finely chopped
2 cloves garlic
1kg (2lb) ripe tomatoes, peeled & finely chopped
25g (1oz) sugar
1½ tbsp sherry vinegar
2 tsp pimentón dulce (sweet paprika)
1 tbsp olive oil
salt & pepper, to taste

1 Fry the onion and garlic in a pan until soft and translucent.

2 Add the chopped tomatoes, and cook until the mixture reduces. Then add the sugar, the vinegar and the *pimentón dulce* along with a glug of olive oil, and simmer for 20 minutes. Blend and season with salt and pepper.

ALIOLI

Traditionally, alioli is made with no eggs, but this is quite difficult to achieve. Increasingly egg yolks are added. For best results, allow all the ingredients to reach room temperature before you begin.

Ingredients
6 cloves garlic, finely chopped
½ tsp salt
2 egg yolks
300ml (10½ fl oz) olive oil
salt, to taste

1 Mash garlic with the salt using a mortar and pestle.

2 Add this paste to the egg yolks and mix well.

3 Slowly add the olive oil while whisking until an emulsion is formed.

4 Add salt to taste.

SOFRITO/SOFREGIT

Ingredients
3 tbsp olive oil
4 medium onions, finely chopped
3 cloves garlic, finely chopped (optional)
8 large tomatoes, finely chopped

1 Heat the olive oil in a pan and add the onions, cooking over a medium heat until caramelised (around 15 minutes). Add the garlic if using.

2 Add the tomatoes, stir well, then simmer over a low heat for an hour until the mixture has reduced by half.

PICADA

There are dozens of variations on this basic sauce, which serves both to thicken and add flavour. If more thickening is required, add a couple of tablespoons of fried breadcrumbs.

Ingredients
20g (¾oz) almonds
20g (¾ oz) hazelnuts
2 cloves garlic, peeled
3 tbsp parsley, chopped
pinch salt
2 tbsp olive oil

1 Blend all the ingredients except the oil in a food processor until the mix resembles a thick paste. Add the oil and stir in well by hand.

RECIPE SOURCES

NORTHEAST SPAIN

1 **Carles Abellan**, Tapas 24, C/Diputació 269, Barcelona (pp10–13) www.carlesabellan.com/ mis-restaurantes/tapas-24 +34 934 88 09 77

2 **Fidel Amigó**, Cal Xim, Sant Pau d'Ordal (pp14–17) www.calxim.com +34 938 99 30 92

3 **María Solivellas**, Ca na Toneta, C/de l'Horitzó 21, Caimari (pp18–21) www.canatoneta.com +34 971 51 52 26

4 **Fina Puigdevall**, Les Cols, Ctra de la Canya s/n, Olot (pp22–5) www.lescols. com +34 972 26 92 09

5 **Manel Marqués**, Suquet de l'Almirall, Passeig de Joan de Borbó 65, Barcelona (pp26–9) www.suquetdelalmirall.com +34 932 21 62 33

6 **Jaume Jovells**, Can Pineda, Carrer de Sant Joan de Malta 55, Barcelona (pp30–33) www.restaurantcanpineda. com +34 933 08 30 81

7 **Alex Múgica**, La Cocina de Alex Múgica, Calle Estafeta 24, Pamplona (pp34–37) www.alexmugica.com +34 948 51 01 25

8 **Jordi Artal**, Cinc Sentits, C/Aribau 58, Barcelona (pp38–43) www.cincsentits.com +34 933 23 94 90

9 **Juan José Banqueri Fernández**, Parrilla Albarracín, Plaza de Nuestra Señora del Carmen, 1-3 (pp44–47) www.parrillaalbarracin.com +34 976 15 81 00

10 **Marc Fosh**, Simply Fosh, Carrer de la Missió 7A, Palma (pp48–51) www. simplyfosh.com +34 971 72 01 14

11 **José Manuel Benito**, Arrocería La Valenciana, Calle Juristes 12, Valencia (pp52–5) www.arrocerialavalenciana. com +34 963 15 38 56

12 **Miquel Calent**, Ca'n Calent, Ronda de l'Estació 44, Campos (pp56–9) www. cancalent.com +34 971 65 14 45

13 **Meri Viladecàs Pascual**, Fussimanya, Ctra Parador km 7 (pp60–3) www.fussimanya.cat +34 938 12 21 88

14 **David Baile Rodríguez**, Restaurante Batiste, Av Fernando Pérez Ojeda 6, Santa Pola (pp64–7) www. restaurantebatiste.es +34 965 41 14 85

15 **Andreu Genestra**, Aromata, C/Concepció 12, Palma (pp68–71) www. aromatarestaurant.com +34 971 49 58 33

16 **Tomeu Arbona**, Fornet de la Soca, C/Sant Jaume 23, Palma (pp72–5) www. fornetdelasoca.com +34 673 49 94 46

17 **Christian Escribà**, Escribà, Rambla de les Flors 83, Barcelona (pp76–79) www.escriba.es +34 933 01 60 27

CENTRAL SPAIN

1 **Paco Roncero**, Estado Puro, Plaza Cánovas del Castillo 4, Madrid (pp82–5) www.tapasenestadopuro.com

2 **Miguel Torrejón Álvarez**, Hospedería de Real Monasterio, Plaza de Su Majestad Juan Carlos I, Guadalupe (pp86–9) www. hotelhospederiamonasterioguadalupe. com +34 927 36 70 00

3 **Cándido López**, Mesón de Cándido, Plaza Azoguejo 5, Segovia (pp90–3) www. mesondecandido.es +34 921 425 911

4 **Adolfo Muñoz Martín**, Adolfo Pasaje Callejón Hombre de Palo, C/Hombre de Palo 7, Toledo (pp94–9) www.adolforestaurante.com, +34 925 22 73 21

5 **Salvador González Alcoholado**, Taberna La Carmencita, Calle de la Libertad 16, Madrid (pp100–103) www.tabernalacarmencita.wordpress. com +34 915 31 09 11

6 **Antonio Sánchez Garcia**, Corral del Rey, Plazuela del Corral del Rey, Trujillo (pp104–7) www.corraldelreytrujillo.com +34 927 32 30 71

7 **Nino Redruello**, La Gabinoteca, C/Fernández de la Hoz 53, Madrid (pp108–11) www.lagabinoteca.com +34 913 99 15 00

8 **Ángel Gómez Caballero**, Figón del Huécar, Ronda Julián Romero 6, Cuenca (pp112–15) www.figondelhuecar.es +34 969 24 00 62

9 **Amparo Moreno**, Casa Ciriaco, Calle Mayor 84, Madrid (pp116–19) +34 915 48 06 20

10 **José Luís Entradas del Barco**, La Rebotica, Calle Boticas 12, Zafra (pp120–3) +34 924 55 42 89

11 **Toño Pérez**, Atrio Restaurante Hotel, Plaza de San Mateo 1, Cáceres (pp124–7) www.restauranteatrio.com +34 927 24 29 28

12 **Alejandro Jarrones Arias**, El Figón de Eustaquio, Plaza San Juan 12-14, Cáceres (pp128–31) www.elfigon deeustaquio.com +34 927 24 43 62

13 **Dolores (Lola) Soto Sánchez**, La Bola, Calle Bola 5, Madrid (pp132–5) www.labola.es +34 915 47 69 30

(14) **Juan Bañez Valerio**, La Parrilla de San Lorenzo, C/Pedro Niño 1, Valladolid (pp136–9) www.parrilladesanlorenzo.es +34 983 33 50 88

(15) **Isabel Hernández Vallejo**, Bollería y Pastelería Mariano Hernández, Plaza Magana 1, Ávila (pp140–3) www.bolleriamarianohernandez.com +34 920 21 29 95

(16) **Daniel Real**, Chocolatería San Ginés, Pasadizo de San Ginés 5, Madrid (pp144–7) www.chocolateriasangines.com +34 913 65 65 46

NORTHWEST SPAIN

(1) **Edorta Lamo**, A Fuego Negro, Calle 31 de Agosto, San Sebastián (pp150–5) www.afuegonegro.com +34 650 13 53 73

(2) **Paula Ale**, La Cuchara de San Telmo, Calle 31 de Agosto 28, San Sebastián (pp156–9) www.lacuchara desantelmo.com +34 943 44 16 55

(3) **Rubén Cirés Molina**, Restaurante Campos, Rúa Nova 2–4, Lugo (pp160–3) www.restaurantecampos.es +34 982 22 97 43

(4) **Pedro Subijana**, Akelarre, Paseo Padre Orcolaga 56, San Sebastián (pp164–7) www.akelarre.net +34 943 31 12 09

(5) **Juan Carlos Caro**, Zelai Txiki, Travesía Rodil 79, Falda de Ulía, San Sebastián (pp168–71) www.restaurant ezelaitxiki.com +34 943 27 46 22

(6) **Francis Paniego**, Tondeluna, C/Muro de Francisco de la Mata 8, Logroño (pp172–5) www.tondeluna.com +34 941 23 64 25

(7) **(14)** **Patricio Fuentes**, San Sebastián Food, Calle Okendo 1, San Sebastián (pp176–9, 204–7) www.sansebastianfood.com +34 943 43 76 00

(8) **Luís Alberto Martínez**, Casa Fermín, C/San Francisco 8, Oviedo (pp176–9) www.casafermin.com +34 985 21 64 52

(9) **Nacho Manzano**, Casa Marcial, La Salgar s/n, Parres (pp180–3) www.casamarcial.com +34 985 84 09 91

(10) **Guillermo Zabala**, Casa Zabala, C/Vizconde de Campo Grande 2, Gijón (pp184–7) www.casazabala.com +34 985 34 17 31

(11) **Jesús Sánchez Sainz**, Cenador de Amós Plaza del Sol s/n, Villaverde de Pontones (pp188–91) www.cenadordeamos.com +34 942 50 82 43

(12) **Javier Montero**, O Tragaluz, Praza de San Miguel dos Agros 9, Santiago de Compostela (pp196–9) www.otragaluz.com +34 881 16 82 28

(13) **Gonzalo Abal Lobato**, O Dezaseis, C/San Pedro 16, A Coruña (pp200–3) www.dezaseis.com +34 981 56 48 80

(15) **Marcos Morán**, Casa Gerardo, Carretera AS-19, km 8.5, Prendes (pp208–11) www.restaurant ecasagerardo.es +34 985 88 77 97

(16) **Koki García**, Mesón de Alberto, Calle de la Cruz 4, Lugo (pp212–15) www.mesondealberto.com +34 982 22 83 10

SOUTH SPAIN

(1) **Gracia Nina**, Antigua Abacería de San Lorenzo, Calle Teodosio 53, Seville (pp218–21) www.antiguaabaceria desanlorenzo.com +34 954 38 00 67

(2) **Daniel Toscano Sotelo**, El Rinconcillo, C/Gerona 2, Seville (pp222–5) www.elrinconcillo.es +34 954 22 31 83

(3) **Jota Leirós**, La Chalá, Plaza de la Puerta Real 6, Seville (pp226–9) +34 954 90 30 91

(4) **Ricardo Núñez Romero**, Casa Ricardo, Calle Hernán Cortés 2, Seville (pp230–3) www.casaricardosevilla.com +34 954 38 97 51

(5) **Fernando Córdoba**, El Faro de El Puerto, Av de Fuenterrabía km. 0.5, El Puerto de Santa María (pp234–7) www.elfarodelpuerto.com +34 956 87 09 52

(6) **Juanjo Ruiz**, La Salmoreteca, Puesto no.7, Mercado Victoria, Paseo Victoria s/n, Córdoba (pp238–41) www.lasalmoreteca.com +34 657 92 45 37

(7) **Juan Gutiérrez Moreno**, Bodegas Campos, C/Lineros 32, Córdoba (pp242–5) www.bodegascampos.com +34 957 49 75 00

(8) **Adelina Pandelet**, Alboronía, Plaza Peones s/n, Jerez de la Frontera (pp246–9) +34 627 99 20 03

(9) **Manu Jara**, Manu Jara, C/Pureza 5, Seville (pp250–5) www.manujara.com +34 675 87 36 74

(10) **Javier Muñoz**, La Carboná, Calle San Francisco de Paula 2, Jerez de la Frontera (pp256–9) +34 956 34 74 75

(11) **Miguel López Hernández**, La Pequeña Taberna, Plaza San Juan 7, Murcia (pp260–3) www.lapequenataberna.com +34 968 21 98 40

INDEX

T

V

ABOUT THE AUTHOR

Sally Davies first set foot on Spanish shores in 1992, where she worked on the Seville Expo and realised that vegetarianism was not, perhaps, the wisest lifestyle choice for Andalucía, and was soon seduced by the Sunday paella ritual; the earthenware ramekins of oxtail stew, flaming chorizo or prawns al ajillo available in every Seville bar; and the exquisite pleasures of a plate of cured acorn-fed ham. For the last 15 years she has lived in Barcelona, writing on Spain and its restaurants for a number of guidebooks, as well as newspapers and magazines including the *Guardian*, the *Daily Telegraph*, the *Observer*, *Wallpaper**, and the *Sunday Times*.

ACKNOWLEDGEMENTS

First and foremost, thanks to the indefatigable Mary-Ann Gallagher for her tenacious pursuit of elusive chefs, and to Ricard Raventos for bringing order to chaos. Thanks too to Margaret Stepien for some unforgettable adventures and so many comic moments. To the ever patient Karyn Noble and the long-suffering Robin Barton at Lonely Planet, and to Stephen Burgen for his cheerful chauffeuring.

Of invaluable assistance were Esther Rojo Barroso at the Spanish Tourist Office in London, Karissa Winters and Yadira Chaparro at the Extremadura tourist board, and Dominique Carroll and Toni Gómez at the Mallorca tourist board. Thanks for some spectacular hotel rooms to Felisa Acedo (www.nh-hotels.com/hotel/nh-trujillo-palacio-de-santa-marta and www.nh-collection.com/hotel/nh-collection-caceres-palacio-de-oquendo) in Extremadura; Vanessa Ferrer (www.hotel-mariacristina.com), Ander Elortegi (www.villasoro.com) and David Cornejo (www.hlondres.com) in San Sebastián; Matilde Villegas (www.dearhotelmadrid.com) and Carlota Romero (www.hotelurso.com) in Madrid; and Juan Segura (www.hotelmonasteriodesanmiguel.es) in El Puerto de Santa María.

For contacts and restaurant ideas, many thanks to Isabella and John Noble, Andy Symington, Annie Bennett, Jon Warren, Fiona Flores Watson, Lotta Jörgensen, Anna O'Flynn, Katherine McLaughlin, Jordi Artal, Paul Richardson, Anna Ripoll Agulló and Pep Planas.

And, of course, all the chefs and their teams, with special mention to Miquel Calent, Fernando Córdoba, Carles Abellan, María Solivellas, Meri Viladecàs Pascual, Pedro Subijana and Andreu Genestra, for opening their little black books to us, ferrying us to train stations, and making invaluable suggestions.

Back in Barcelona, thanks to my parents, Sarah Davison, Matthew Wrigley, Cathy Runciman and John O'Donovan for babysitting, cat-sitting and generally keeping the home fires burning. And, most of all, thanks to Tess, for her understanding and good cheer in the face of my long hours and frequent absences.

ABOUT THE PHOTOGRAPHER

Polish hardware, Canadian software and a Spanish IP for the past 15 years are the essential ingredients that produce the photographer-stylist cocktail that is Margaret Stepien. With this mix of contrasting cultural influences, Margaret feels comfortable shooting in almost any environment, always aiming to capture the beauty and unique nature of any subject that happens to appear before her lens, whether it be a plate of Iberico ham or the Duchess of Wales. Client demands in the past few years have directed her career to focus on the food and beverage sector. She has recently completed campaigns for such companies as KFC, Danone, Asturiana, VIPS, Estrella Damm, Biossance, a book on Barcelona's Boqueria Market, travel articles for Lonely Planet, P&O magazines, and *Marie Claire*, among many others.

ACKNOWLEDGEMENTS

I have to say the most satisfying part of this project has been working with such a fantastic team. It has been a real pleasure to share the adventures and meals with Sally Davies who, apart from being great company has also been amazing at sorting out the logistics of such a large and complicated project. A big warm thank you to my boyfriend Antonio, whose support eased the craziness of six months of travel, and who also kept the cat alive. They are too many to mention, but I'd like to thank all the wonderful chefs whose hospitality has led me to an even deeper appreciation of the cultural and gastronomic diversity of this wonderful country. And thanks, of course, to everyone from Lonely Planet who planted the seed and brought this project to fruition.

Published in September 2016 by Lonely Planet Global Limited
CRN 554153
www.lonelyplanet.com
ISBN 978 1 76034 0766
© Lonely Planet 2016
Printed in China
Written by Sally Davies
Photographed by Margaret Stepien

Publishing Director Piers Pickard
Associate Publisher & Commissioning Editor Robin Barton
Art Direction Daniel Di Paolo
Layout Designer Lauren Egan
Illustrator Louise Sheeran
Copyeditor Karyn Noble
Cartographers Anita Banh, Corey Hutchinson, Wayne Murphy
Pre-press Production Ryan Evans
Print Production Larissa Frost, Nigel Longuet

Thanks to Mary-Ann Gallagher, Ricard Raventos

With thanks to the recipe testers: Rebecca Law, Amy Lysen, Tracy Whitmey, Grainne Quinn, Jean-Pierre Masclef, Clive Shepherd & Luna Soo, Alex MacLeish, Rick Wiebusch, Adam Bennett & Michael Palmer, Sophie Barton, Christine Barton

Lonely Planet offices

AUSTRALIA
The Malt Store, Level 3, 551 Swanston Street, Carlton VIC, 3053 Australia
Phone 03 8379 8000

USA
150 Linden St, Oakland, CA 94607
Phone 510 250 6400

UNITED KINGDOM
240 Blackfriars Road, London SE1 8NW
Phone 020 3771 5100

IRELAND
Unit E, Digital Court, The Digital Hub, Rainsford St,
Dublin 8, Ireland

STAY IN TOUCH lonelyplanet.com/contact

Paper in this book is certified against the Forest Stewardship Council™ standards. FSC™ promotes environmentally responsible, socially beneficial and economically viable management of the world's forests.